RETIREMENT ISSUES, PLANS AND LIFESTYLES

401(K) PLANS

PROTECTION ISSUES FOR FORCED TRANSFERS AND INACTIVE ACCOUNTS

RETIREMENT ISSUES, PLANS AND LIFESTYLES

Additional books in this series can be found on Nova's website under the Series tab.

Additional e-books in this series can be found on Nova's website under the e-book tab.

RETIREMENT ISSUES, PLANS AND LIFESTYLES

401(K) PLANS

PROTECTION ISSUES FOR FORCED TRANSFERS AND INACTIVE ACCOUNTS

SUZANNE ABBOTT

EDITOR

nova publishers

New York

Library of Congress Cataloging-in-Publication Data

ISBN: 978-1-63482-598-6

Published by Nova Science Publishers, Inc. † New York

CONTENTS

PREFACE

Millions of employees change jobs each year and some leave their savings in their former employers' 401(k) plans. If their accounts are small enough and they do not instruct the plan to do otherwise, plans can transfer their savings into an IRA without their consent. The United States Government Accountability Office examined the implications for 401(k) plan participants of being forced out of plans and into these IRAs. This book examines what happens over time to the savings of participants forced out of their plans; the challenges 401(k) plan participants face keeping track of retirement savings in general; and how other countries address similar challenges of inactive accounts. This book also discusses the issues plan sponsors, fiduciaries, service providers, and other parties face in handling plan benefits payable to participants and beneficiaries who cannot be found or are nonresponsive.

Chapter 1 - Millions of employees change jobs each year and some leave their savings in their former employers' 401(k) plans. If their accounts are small enough and they do not instruct the plan to do otherwise, plans can transfer their savings into an IRA without their consent. GAO was asked to examine implications for 401(k) plan participants of being forced out of plans and into these IRAs.

GAO examined: (1) what happens over time to the savings of participants forced out of their plans, (2) the challenges 401(k) plan participants face keeping track of retirement savings in general, and (3) how other countries address similar challenges of inactive accounts. GAO's review included projecting forced-transfer IRA outcomes over time using current fee and return data from 10 providers, and interviews with stakeholders in the United States, Australia, Belgium, Denmark, the Netherlands, Switzerland, and the United Kingdom.

Chapter 2 - The 2013 ERISA Advisory Council ("Council") examined the issues plan sponsors, fiduciaries, service providers, and other parties ("Plan Representatives") face in handling plan benefits payable to participants and beneficiaries who cannot be found or are nonresponsive ("Lost Participants"). The focus of the Council's examination was on both methods of maintaining contact with participants so they do not become Lost Participants and methods of finding participants once they become Lost Participants.

The Council learned from witnesses who testified that locating Lost Participants to pay them their benefits can be an administrative burden. Further, while there is DOL guidance on dealing with Lost Participants, that guidance is (i) focused on terminated defined contribution plans, (ii) presented in multiple sources rather than one central and cohesive resource, or (iii) outdated. Furthermore, there does not appear to be sufficient inter-agency coordination among the DOL, the Pension Benefit Guaranty Corporation, and the Social Security Administration to address overlapping issues surrounding Lost Participants. The Council makes several recommendations in this report regarding how to address each of these findings.

Chapter 3 - Testimony of John A. Turner, Director, Pension Policy Center.

In: 401(k) Plans
Editor: Suzanne Abbott

ISBN: 978-1-63482-598-6

Chapter 1

401(K) PLANS: GREATER PROTECTIONS NEEDED FOR FORCED TRANSFERS AND INACTIVE ACCOUNTS*

United States Government Accountability Office

WHY GAO DID THIS STUDY

Millions of employees change jobs each year and some leave their savings in their former employers' 401(k) plans. If their accounts are small enough and they do not instruct the plan to do otherwise, plans can transfer their savings into an IRA without their consent. GAO was asked to examine implications for 401(k) plan participants of being forced out of plans and into these IRAs.

GAO examined: (1) what happens over time to the savings of participants forced out of their plans, (2) the challenges 401(k) plan participants face keeping track of retirement savings in general, and (3) how other countries address similar challenges of inactive accounts. GAO's review included projecting forced-transfer IRA outcomes over time using current fee and return data from 10 providers, and interviews with stakeholders in the United States, Australia, Belgium, Denmark, the Netherlands, Switzerland, and the United Kingdom.

* This is an edited, reformatted and augmented version of a United States Government Accountability Office publication, No. GAO-15-73, dated November 2014.

WHAT GAO RECOMMENDS

GAO recommends that Congress consider (1) amending current law to permit alternative default destinations for plans to use when transferring participant accounts out of plans, and (2) repealing a provision that allows plans to disregard rollovers when identifying balances eligible for transfer to an IRA. Among other things, GAO also recommends that DOL convene a taskforce to explore the possibility of establishing a national pension registry. DOL and SSA each disagreed with one of GAO's recommendations. GAO maintains the need for all its recommendations.

WHAT GAO FOUND

When a participant has saved less than $5,000 in a 401(k) plan and changes jobs without indicating what should be done with the money, the plan can transfer the account savings—a forced transfer—into an individual retirement account (IRA). Savings in these IRAs are intended to be preserved by the conservative investments allowed under Department of Labor (DOL) regulations. However, GAO found that because fees outpaced returns in most of the IRAs analyzed, these account balances tended to decrease over time. Without alternatives to forced-transfer IRAs, current law permits billions in participant savings to be poorly invested for the long-term. GAO also found that a provision in law allows a plan to disregard previous rollovers when determining if a balance is small enough to force out. For example, a plan can force out a participant with a balance of $20,000 if less than $5,000 is attributable to contributions other than rollover contributions.

Some 401(k) plan participants find it difficult to keep track of their savings, particularly when they change jobs, because of challenges with consolidation, communication, and information. First, individuals who accrue multiple accounts over the course of a career may be unable to consolidate their accounts by rolling over savings from one employer's plan to the next. Second, maintaining communication with a former employer's plan can be challenging if companies are restructured and plans are terminated or merged and renamed. Third, key information on lost accounts may be held by different plans, service providers, or government agencies, and participants may not know where to turn for assistance. Although the Social Security Administration provides individuals with information on benefits they may have from former employers' plans, the information is not provided in a consolidated or timely manner that would be useful to recipients.

The six countries GAO reviewed address challenges of inactive accounts by using forced transfers that help preserve account value and providing a variety of tracking tools referred to as pension registries. For example, officials in two countries told GAO that inactive accounts are consolidated there by law, without participant consent, in money-making investment vehicles. Officials in the United Kingdom said that it consolidates savings in a participant's new plan and in Switzerland such savings are invested together in a single fund. In Australia, small, inactive accounts are held by a federal agency that preserves their real value by regulation until they are claimed. In addition, GAO found that Australia, the Netherlands and Denmark have pension registries, not always established by law or regulation, which provide participants a single source of online information on their new and old retirement accounts.

Participants in the United States, in contrast, often lack the information needed to keep track of their accounts. No single agency has responsibility for consolidating retirement account information for participants, and so far, the pension industry has not taken on the task. Without a pension registry for individuals to access current, consolidated retirement account information, the challenges participants face in tracking accounts over time can be expected to continue.

ABBREVIATIONS

ATO	Australian Tax Office
BLS	Bureau of Labor Statistics
DOL	Department of Labor
EBSA	Employee Benefit Security Administration
EGTRRA	Economic Growth and Tax Relief Reconciliation Act of 2001
ERISA	Employee Retirement Income Security Act of 1974
IRA	individual retirement account
IRC	Internal Revenue Code
IRS	Internal Revenue Service
OEA	Office of Outreach, Education, and Assistance
PBGC	Pension Benefit Guaranty Corporation
PPA	Pension Protection Act of 2006
SEC	Securities and Exchange Commission

SSA Social Security Administration
Treasury Department of the Treasury

* * *

November 21, 2014

The Honorable Tom Harkin
Chairman
Committee on Health, Education, Labor and Pensions
United States Senate

The Honorable Elizabeth Warren
Member
Committee on Health, Education, Labor and Pensions
United States Senate

Every year, millions of American workers change jobs[1] and many fail to stipulate what should be done with 401(k) plan[2] savings[3] they may have accrued. If a separated participant's[4] 401(k) plan balance is small enough, it can be transferred out of the plan. Specifically, the Internal Revenue Code[5] allows former employers to force participants with vested balances of $5,000 or less out of their 401(k) plans[6] and, absent participant instruction, transfer their savings into an individual retirement account (IRA) referred to as a forced-transfer[7] IRA in this report. Despite the potentially large volume of forced transfers that may occur annually, their effects on workers' retirement security are not well understood.[8] Additionally, many employees go on to participate in other companies' 401(k) plans and may accumulate multiple accounts over time. As these employees continue to move in and out of jobs, companies go out of business or merge with other companies, and plans are terminated or merged as a part of corporate restructuring, it is difficult for plans and participants to keep track of one another, according to industry professionals and consumer groups.

Regulators have focused on helping plan participants save through 401(k) plans, but little attention has been paid to the use of forced transfers or managing multiple accounts. Consequently, you asked us to examine these issues and the steps that other countries may be taking to address similar issues. Specifically, this report examines (1) what happens to forced-transfer IRAs over time, (2) the challenges 401(k) plan participants face keeping track of their retirement savings, and what, if anything, is being done to help them, and (3) how other countries address the challenges of inactive[9] accounts.

To understand what happens to forced-transfer IRAs over time as well as challenges 401(k) plan participants face keeping track of multiple 401(k) plan accounts, we reviewed relevant data from government, research, and industry sources. Because we found no comprehensive data on the number of IRA accounts opened as a result of forced transfers or other data relevant to their use and management, we collected data from a non-generalizeable group of 10 providers of forced-transfer IRAs about their practices and outcomes, including 3 of the largest IRA providers. There is no comprehensive list of all forced-transfer IRA providers. For this reason, we built a list of them through interviews with industry professionals, a review of IRA market data, and online searches. Our objective was to create a group that would cover a large share of assets in the forced-transfer IRA market and represent both small and large IRA providers in terms of company size. We reached out to the largest IRA providers by assets under management, as well as all small forced-transfer IRA providers on our list and obtained forced-transfer IRA account data from 10 providers that represent this mix of characteristics. We also interviewed plan sponsor groups, 401(k) plan industry groups, research entities, consumer groups, and six federal agencies (Consumer Financial Protection Bureau, Department of Labor, Department of the Treasury, Pension Benefit Guaranty Corporation, Securities and Exchange Commission, and Social Security Administration) about plans' use of forced transfers and what challenges individuals and plans face related to inactive accounts and multiple 401(k) plan accounts in the United States. To assess the reliability of the data we analyzed, we reviewed IRA market data and interviewed IRA providers familiar with forced-transfer IRAs. We determined that these data were sufficiently reliable for the purposes of this report.

We also reviewed research and industry literature, relevant federal laws and regulations, Advisory Council on Employee Welfare and Pension Benefit Plans[10] testimony on missing participants, industry whitepapers on a proposed default roll-in system, and submissions in response to the 2013 Pension Benefit Guaranty Corporation request for information related to a tracking system for distributions from terminating plans.

To examine how some countries are addressing the challenges of inactive retirement accounts, we selected six countries to study. In making our selection we considered countries with extensive workplace retirement systems to include populations that might face challenges similar to those of U.S. participants, and considered the extent to which such countries had recent or innovative approaches to address the challenges posed by inactive retirement accounts. We determined that six countries could potentially provide lessons for the United States. They were Australia, Belgium, Denmark, the Netherlands, Switzerland, and the United Kingdom. We interviewed government officials, service providers, and other stakeholders from all the selected countries. We did not conduct an independent legal analysis to verify the information provided about the laws or regulations in the countries we selected for this study. Instead, we relied on appropriate secondary sources, interviews with relevant officials, and other sources to support our work. We submitted key report excerpts to agency officials in each country for their review and verification, and we incorporated their technical corrections as necessary. Appendix I provides additional information on our scope and methodology.

We conducted this performance audit from May 2013 to November 2014 in accordance with generally accepted government auditing standards. Those standards require that we plan and perform the audit to obtain sufficient, appropriate evidence to provide a reasonable basis for our findings and conclusions based on our audit objectives. We believe that the evidence obtained provides a reasonable basis for our findings and conclusions based on our audit objectives.

BACKGROUND

Forced Transfers and Forced-Transfer IRAs

A forced transfer occurs when a plan participant has separated from an employer, but still has vested savings in the employer's 401(k) plan and the plan sponsor decides not to allow the savings to remain in the plan. Prior to the Economic Growth and Tax Relief Reconciliation Act of 2001 (EGTRRA),[11] plans could, in the absence of participant instructions, distribute balances of not more than $5,000 by paying them directly to the participant, referred to as a cash-out. EGTRRA sought to protect forced-out participants' retirement savings by requiring that, in the absence of participant instructions, active plans transfer balances of $1,000 or more to forced-transfer IRAs, thus permitting the plan to distribute them while preserving their tax-preferred status.[12] Expanding upon the statute, regulations later provided that in the absence of participant instructions, plans could opt to also transfer balances of $1,000 or less into forced-transfer IRAs. Active plans may not distribute accounts with contributions of more than $5,000 without the consent of the participant.[13]

EGTRRA also required DOL to prescribe regulations providing safe harbors under which the designation of a provider and the investment of funds for a forced-transfer IRA are deemed to satisfy fiduciary duties under ERISA.[14] These regulations, issued in 2004, established a 'safe harbor' for plan fiduciaries transferring forced-out participants' accounts, which includes conditions pertaining to the plan fiduciaries' selection of the IRA provider and the investments of the transferred funds.[15] We identified five main components in the regulations, which are: (1) preservation of principal, (2) maintenance of the dollar value of the investment, (3) using an investment product of a state or federally regulated financial institution, (4) fees and expenses, and (5) a participant's right to enforce the terms of the IRA. Plan sponsors forcing participants out of plans by transferring their accounts into forced-transfer IRAs legally satisfy their fiduciary standard of care to participants if they comply with DOL's safe harbor regulations.[16] After the account is transferred into a forced-transfer IRA it is subject to the rules generally governing IRAs.

A forced-transfer IRA is a type of IRA that can be opened by a plan on behalf of a participant, without the specific consent or cooperation of that participant. In these instances, a plan signs a contract with an IRA provider, which may or may not be the plan's record keeper, to establish and maintain the account. While the use of forced-transfer IRAs for accounts under $1,000 is not required, plan sponsors may elect to use forced-transfer IRAs rather than cash-outs when forcing out such accounts in the absence of distribution instructions from the participant, as shown in figure 1.[17]

Use of forced-transfer IRAs is common among 401(k) plans. One annual industry survey shows that about half of active 401(k) plans force out separated participants with balances of $1,000 to $5,000.[18]

Data provided by the Social Security Administration (SSA) highlight an amount of retirement savings that could be eligible for forced-transfer IRAs. From 2004 through 2013, separated employees left more than 16 million accounts of $5,000 or less in workplace plans, with an aggregate value of $8.5 billion.[19] A portion of those accounts constitutes billions in retirement savings that could be transferred later to IRAs. Even if plans do not force out participants' accounts immediately upon separation they may do so later in the year. For instance, they may sweep out small accounts of separated participants once a year or amend their plans years after participants separate and then force them out.

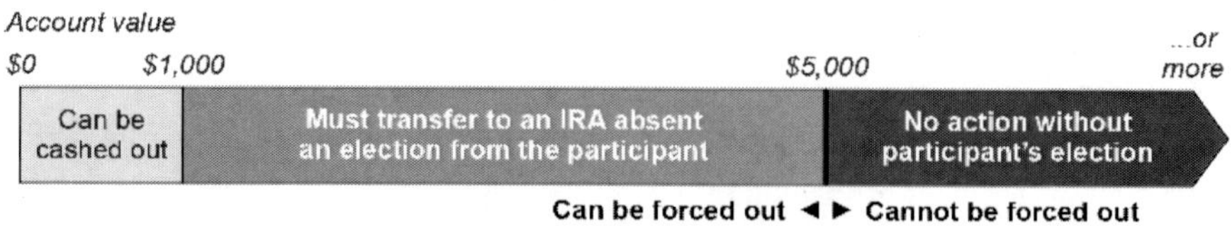

Source: GAO review of select laws and regulations. | GAO-15-73.

Note: A plan can only transfer a participant's eligible account to a forced-transfer IRA in the absence of the participant's instruction to do otherwise. An account of less than $1,000 can also be transferred to a forced-transfer IRA, if the plan provides. These balance thresholds pertain to active plans. In the case of terminating plans that must distribute all benefits in order to complete the termination, plans can forcibly transfer missing participants' account balances of any size if the participant, after being notified, does not provide instruction and cannot be located after a search.

Figure 1. Options for Forcing Out a Separated Participant Depend on the Participant's Vested Balance.

Regulatory Oversight of Forced Transfers

Multiple federal agencies have a role in overseeing forced transfers and investments, inside and outside the Employee Retirement Income Security Act of 1974 (ERISA) plan environment, as discussed in table 1.

Table 1. Brief Summary of Federal Agencies' Roles Overseeing Forced Transfers of Separated 401(k) Plan Participants

Department of Labor (DOL)	DOL administers and enforces the Employee Retirement Income Security Act of 1974 (ERISA), which requires plan fiduciaries to act solely in the interest of plan participants and beneficiaries.[a] DOL promulgated a safe harbor rule pursuant to statute[b] for plans transferring balances to forced-transfer IRAs.[c] The rule sets out conditions that, if met, will ensure that a plan sponsor using forced-transfer IRAs satisfies its fiduciary standard of care under ERISA. Like the plan sponsor, DOL's oversight of such funds generally ends after those funds are transferred out of the ERISA plan into a forced-transfer IRA because DOL generally has no jurisdiction over IRAs.[d]

Internal Revenue Service (IRS)	The IRS oversees the compliance of 401(k) plans and IRAs with the Internal Revenue Code (IRC), which sets standards plans and IRAs must meet to qualify for preferential tax treatment. For example, the IRC lays out requirements for plans making forced transfers[e] and requires that any participant whose balance is to be distributed has the option of having a direct (and thus, non-taxable) transfer of their balance to a tax-qualified plan or IRA of their choosing. The IRS is also responsible for imposing taxes on prohibited transactions.[f]
Pension Benefit Guaranty Corporation (PBGC)	The Pension Protection Act of 2006 amended ERISA to require PBGC to expand its program under which terminated defined benefit plans must transfer the designated benefits of missing participants to PBGC, to permit terminating 401(k) plans to transfer the assets of missing participants to PBGC as well.[g] On June 21, 2013, the agency published a request for information from the public about how to implement the new requirement,[h] but has not yet implemented it. PBGC may, but is not required to, compel terminating defined contribution plans to provide information on what happens to participant accounts. PBGC does not track information about the location of assets transferred out of active plans into forced-transfer IRAs, but maintains an online database the public can use to find lost benefits from some terminated defined benefit plans.
Social Security Administration (SSA)	SSA maintains data reported to the IRS by plans on undistributed vested 401(k) plan (and other plan) benefits of their separated participants using the Form 8955-SSA.[i] When individuals apply for Social Security benefits, SSA must transmit to the individuals, on a letter called "Potential Private Retirement Benefit Information,"[j] notice that the individuals may be entitled to private retirement savings or benefits from a past employer.

Securities and Exchange Commission (SEC)	The laws that govern the securities industry include the Securities Act of 1933, the Securities Exchange Act of 1934, the Investment Company Act of 1940 and the Investment Advisers Act of 1940.[k] The SEC is the primary regulator overseeing various entities (e.g., transfer agents broker-dealers) and investment vehicles, such as mutual funds, which are offered in both 401(k) plans and IRAs. The Investment Company Act of 1940 is the primary law that governs a mutual fund's activities. Mutual funds are subject to extensive investment restrictions and disclosure requirements with respect to risks, fees, and expenses.

Source: GAO review of select laws and regulations. | GAO-15-73

[a] 29 U.S.C. § 1104.

[b] Economic Growth and Tax Relief Reconciliation Act of 2001, Pub. L. No. 107-16, § 657(c)(2), 115 Stat. 38, 136.

[c] 29 C.F.R. § 2550.404a-2.

[d] DOL also determines when prohibited transactions may have occurred with respect to such IRAs.

[e] 26 U.S.C. § 401(a)(31)(B). By distribution, we mean that retirement savings are leaving a particular plan. They could be transferred by the account holder to a new employer's plan, to an existing IRA, or transferred by the plan into a forced-transfer IRA on behalf of the account holder. The distribution could also be cashed out by the account holder—or by the plan if the balance is below $1,000—but in this report we do not assume that a distribution is equivalent to a cash-out.

[f] 26 U.S.C. § 4975.

[g] Pub. L. No. 109-280, § 410(b), 120 Stat. 780, 934-35 (codified at 29 U.S.C. § 1350(d)).

[h] Missing Participants in Individual Account Plans, 78 Fed. Reg. 37,598.

[i] 26 U.S.C. § 6057(a).

[j] 42 U.S.C. §1320b-1(a)(2)(B). See figure 7 for an excerpt of the Notice. The law also requires that SSA provide potential pension benefit information to participants upon request.

[k] 15 U.S.C. §§ 77a - 77bbb, 15 U.S.C. §§ 78a - 78pp, 15 U.S.C. §§ 80a-1 - 80a-64, and 15 U.S.C. §§ 80b-1 - 80b-2, respectively.

CURRENT LAW AND REGULATIONS ALLOW SPONSORS TO FORCE CERTAIN PARTICIPANTS OUT OF 401(K) PLANS, WHICH CAN RESULT IN REDUCED RETIREMENT INCOME

Conservative Investments Required by DOL Can Result in Decreasing Balances in Forced-Transfer IRAs

Some forced-transfer IRAs are not the short-term investment vehicles for which their default investments are better suited, but providers do not have the flexibility under current DOL safe harbor regulations to use investment vehicles that are better suited to a longer-term investment horizon.[20] Rather, the safe harbor requires that the investment "seek to maintain, over the term of the investment," the dollar value equal to the amount rolled over.[21] To achieve this, DOL narrowly wrote the investment guidance portion of the forced-transfer IRA safe harbor regulations to effectively limit providers to holding the funds in money market funds, certificates of deposit, or assets with similarly low investment risk typically deemed appropriate for holding money for a short term.[22] While such conservative investments generally ensure that the money is liquid (that is, available to the owner upon demand for cash-out, transfers to another account, or reinvestment elsewhere), they can result in a low return and potentially minimal growth over time.

Most forced-transfer IRA balances in accounts we analyzed will decrease if not transferred out of forced-transfer IRAs and reinvested, because the fees charged to the forced-transfer IRAs often outpace the low returns earned by the conservative investments prescribed by DOL's safe harbor regulations. In recent years, the typical forced-transfer IRA investment, such as a money market account, has earned almost no return. For example, taxable money market funds averaged 1.45 percent for the 10 years ending July 31, 2014.[23] We collected forced-transfer IRA account information from 10 forced-transfer IRA providers, including information about the fees they charged, the default investments used, and the returns obtained (prior to these fees).[24] Among those 10, there were 19 different combinations of fees and returns, as some providers offered more than one combination for their forced-transfer IRA contracts. The typical investment return for the 19 different forced-transfer IRA combinations ranged from 0.01 percent to 2.05 percent. A low return coupled with administrative fees, ranging from $0 to $100 or more[25] to open the account and $0 to $115 annually, can steadily decrease a comparatively small stagnant balance.[26] Using the forced-transfer IRA fee and investment return combinations, we projected the effects on a $1,000 balance over time. While projections for different fees and returns show balances decreasing at different rates, generally the dynamic was the same: small accounts with low returns and annual fees decline in value, often rapidly. In particular, we found that 13 of the 19 balances decreased to $0 within 30 years.[27] (See appendix III for all projected outcomes.) For example, the fees and investment returns of one provider we interviewed would reduce an unclaimed $1,000 balance to $0 in 9 years.[28] Even if an account holder claimed their forced-transfer IRA after a few years the balance would have significantly decreased. Among the 19 combinations we analyzed, our analysis showed an average decrease in a $1,000 account balance of about 25 percent over just 5 years. The rate of investment return needed to ensure a forced-transfer IRA balance does not lose real value varies depending on the rate of inflation and the fees charged. For example, given the median fees for the 19 forced-transfer IRAs we analyzed, the investment return on $1,000 would have to be more than 7.3 percent to keep pace with both the rate of inflation and the fees charged.[29] Our projections are consistent with anecdotal evidence obtained from forced-transfer IRA providers, five of which told us that their accounts are reduced to zero or do not keep pace with inflation and fees.

Default investments used by many plans for automatic enrollment in 401(k) plans produce a better long-term return than the conservative default investments for forced-transfer IRAs. The most popular default investments for automatic enrollment in 401(k) plans are target date funds. Target date funds, which are often mutual funds, hold a mix of stocks, bonds, and other investments. Over time, the mix gradually shifts according to the fund's investment strategy. We previously reported that target date funds are designed to perform well over a long period of time.[30] As noted in an industry research paper, while some target date funds produced severe losses in 2008, most have since produced double digit gains.[31] In recent years, assets in target date fund default investments have produced a higher return than typical forced-transfer IRA investments, which have seen minimal returns.[32] For example, as shown in figure 2, under reasonable return assumptions, if a forced-out participant's $1,000 forced-transfer IRA balance was invested in a target date fund the balance could grow to about $2,700 over 30 years (173 percent growth), while the balance would decline to $0 if it had been invested in a money market account. We also projected the remaining balance assuming a 15-year average return for money market funds, which is 1.89 percent, and found no material difference in the result. Using that return the balance significantly decreased over time, leaving a $67 balance after 30 years.

According to DOL officials, the agency has the flexibility under current law to expand the safe harbor investment options for forced-transfer IRAs, but currently its regulations do not permit those accounts to be invested in the same funds allowed for participants automatically enrolled in 401(k) plans.[33] DOL's goal of preserving principal is important and consistent with statute, but without more aggressive investment options, forced-transfer IRA balances can continue to lose value over time, causing some former participants to lose the savings they had accumulated in their 401(k) plans. However, allowing forced-transfer IRAs to be invested for growth, such as through a target date fund, may be more effective in preserving principal.

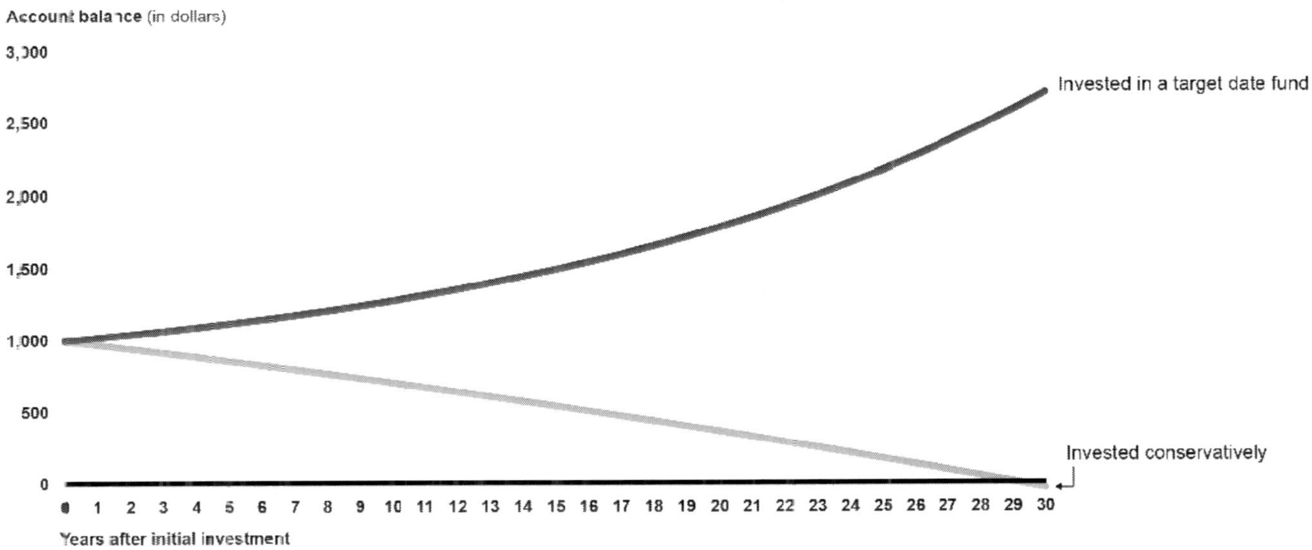

Source: GAO projection based on analysis of investment return data. | GAO-15-73.

Notes: The forced-transfer IRA account assumptions used are the median account opening fee ($6.75), median annual fee ($42), and the mean return on taxable money market funds (1.45 percent) over 10 years ending July 31, 2014. The target date fund example uses the same account fees but reflects a 6.3 percent return, which is the geometric mean of 10 year average returns across all target date funds, ending July 31, 2014. Investment returns reflect our analysis of data reported by Morningstar.com. An alternate projection using the 15 year mean return ending July 31, 2014 on taxable money market funds, which is 1.89 percent, found a result similar to the 10-year return, the funds invested conservatively decreased significantly to $67 after 30 years.

Figure 2. A $1,000 Forced-Transfer IRA Balance Invested in a Target Date Fund Could Grow Over 30 Years but Declines When Invested Conservatively.

Current Law Limits Forced Transfer Options and Permits Plans to Force Out Some Participants with Balances Larger Than $5,000

DOL and IRS Are Precluded from Permitting Alternative Destinations for Forced Transfers

Currently the default destination for forced transfers of more than $1,000 from active plans is an IRA. EGTRRA sought to protect forced-out participants by providing that, in the absence of any participant instructions, active plans that choose to force out participants with accounts of $1,000 or more must transfer the accounts to an individual retirement plan, which is defined as an IRA or individual retirement annuity.[34] Directing these larger balances to IRAs in lieu of cashing them out preserves their savings' tax-preferred status in a retirement account. Current law does not permit DOL and IRS to adopt alternative destinations.

The forced-transfer IRA, like any IRA, is an investment product sold in the retail environment by financial service firms. 35 IRAs are also subject to regulation by the IRS, which oversees contributions to and distributions from them. DOL has limited regulatory oversight over IRAs beyond working with IRS to oversee enforcement of prohibited transactions provisions.[36] Thus, when an individual's 401(k) plan account is transferred to a forced-transfer IRA it is no longer under the regulatory purview of ERISA and is essentially without DOL oversight. In addition, by transferring forced out participants' funds in accordance with the safe harbor regulations, a plan satisfies its fiduciary duty of care under ERISA, and the transfer constitutes a final break between the plan and the transferred account. For example, the plan is not required to monitor the forced-transfer IRA to ensure that the provider abides by the terms of the agreement.

Current law permits terminating plans to distribute forced transfers in multiple ways, with the forced-transfer IRA being only one option, as shown in table 2.[37] In addition to transferring accounts to a forced-transfer IRA, terminating plans may also purchase an annuity with the forced-transfer balances or escheat (transfer) the balances to the state. Further, the Pension Protection Act of 2006 (PPA) created a forthcoming alternative for terminating 401(k) plans, which will be to transfer balances to the Pension Benefit Guaranty Corporation (PBGC) when there are no instructions from the participants.[38] Moreover, we found that some providers will not provide forced-transfer IRAs for terminating plans, generally doing so only as an accommodation to ongoing plan clients and because these plans do not have alternatives to the IRA. As a result, a smaller number of participants forced out of terminating plans will end up with savings in a forced-transfer IRA.

Table 2. Terminating 401(k) Plans Have More Options Than Active Plans When Forcing Out Participants Who Do Not Elect a Distribution Option

	Terminating plans	Active plans
If the participant does not elect another distribution option…	May force out both current and separated participants with balances of any size.	May force out separated participants with balances not in excess of $5,000.
Cash-out (i.e. issue a check to the account holder)	Not an option, unless payment can be reliably made to participant (not in the event of a missing participant).	May cash-out balances of $1,000 or less.
Forced-transfer IRA	May transfer balances of any size to a forced-transfer IRA.	Must transfer accounts of more than $1,000 to $5,000 to a forced-transfer IRA.a Maytransfer accounts of $1,000 or less to a forced-transfer IRA instead of cash out.
Escheat to the stateb	May escheat balances of any size to the participant's last known state of residence or work location, if state requirements are met and if an individual retirement plan is not available.b	Not an option.c
Purchase an annuity	May purchase an annuity for the participant.	An individual retirement annuity is permitted for forced transfers.
Transfer to a bank	May transfer to a federally insured bank account, if an IRA or individual retirement annuity is not available.d	Not an option.
Transfer to Pension Benefit Guaranty Corporation (PBGC)	Pending: May transfer balances of any size to PBGC.	Not an option.

Source: GAO review of select laws and regulations. | GAO-15-73

[a] An IRA is one form of an individual retirement plan. 26 U.S.C. § 7701(a)(37).

[b] States generally have jurisdiction over unclaimed property, but they cannot require escheatment of inactive accounts still in a 401(k) plan because the Employee Retirement Income Security Act of 1974 (ERISA)—the law governing employer-

based retirement plans—preempts states' claims to what would otherwise be considered abandoned property. 29 U.S.C. §1144. Therefore, this escheatment is the plan's choice for the disposition of the account. U.S. Dept. of Labor, Field Assistance Bulletin 2014-01 (Aug. 14, 2014), available at http://www.dol.gov/ebsa/regs/fab2014-1.html.

[c] In testimony before the ERISA Advisory Council, June 4, 2013, a representative of The Plan Sponsor Council of America proposed that escheatment be available to active plans seeking to manage the administrative burden of small inactive accounts.

[d] U.S. Dept. of Labor, Field Assistance Bulletin, 2001-01. Forced-transfer IRAs providers told us that the accounts are sometimes escheated to states after the account holder reaches the age of required minimum distribution.

We also found that forced-transfer IRAs can become long-term investments for the many account holders who do not claim their accounts even though the emphasis placed by the safe harbor regulations on liquidity and minimizing risk are more often associated with short-term investment vehicles. One of the larger providers we interviewed said that during the first year after an account is opened about 30 percent of account holders will do nothing with the account.

According to a forced-transfer IRA service provider, an estimated half of the accounts they opened are for missing participants. Many unclaimed accounts may remain so indefinitely. For example, one provider we interviewed reported that nearly 70 percent of the accounts it has opened within the last 5 years remain open and unclaimed. Additionally, an individual could end up with multiple forced-transfer IRAs over time— each incurring its own administrative fees. Two providers we interviewed explained that they do not consolidate forced-transfer IRAs opened for the same individual, meaning that accounts even with the same provider could incur redundant fees.

Although there may be alternatives to the forced-transfer IRA today that were not considered in 2001 when the law was passed, without authority to do so, DOL and IRS cannot identify or facilitate alternative destinations for these accounts. Providing an alternative destination for forced transfers would help to preserve participants' accounts and increase the possibility for growth. Absent the allowance of such an alternative, as we have shown, former plan participants' savings will continue to be placed in investments unlikely to be preserved or grow over the long term.[39]

Disregarding Rollovers Makes It Harder for Low-Wage Workers to Keep Retirement Savings in a 401(k) Plan

Current law allows plans that are determining if they can force out a participant to exclude rollover amounts and any investment returns that have been earned while in the plan.[40] The law explicitly permits plans to exclude a participant's savings that were rolled into the plan when calculating their vested balance, which determines whether the participant may be forced out. Specifically, separated participants with 401(k) accounts of any size can be forced from a plan if the vested balance (in the absence of rollover amounts and its earnings) is $5,000 or less, as demonstrated in figure 3. A rollover of more than $5,000 would not have been subject to forced transfer if it had remained in the participant's last plan, but may become subject to it once transferred to the new plan.

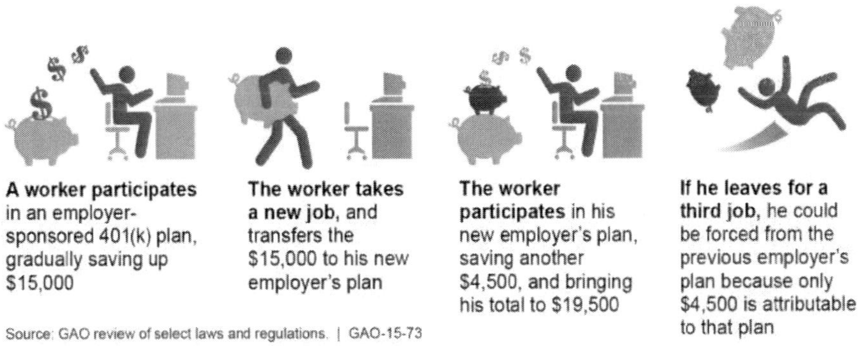

Figure 3. 401(k) Plan Savings Rolled into a New Employer's Plan Are Not Protected by the $5,000 Cap on Forced Transfers.

As discussed further in appendix II, a significant number of plan participants separate from jobs with vested balances at or below $5,000 and thus can be forced out of plans. Many highly mobile workers who participate in 401(k) plans could have significant rollover balances that they have accumulated over time due to successive job changes. However, they could still have their savings transferred out of their plans into forced-transfer IRAs if their plans use forced transfers because they are unlikely to have accumulated $5,000 *vested balances* at their new plans before they separate from employment. Figure 4 shows that disregarding rollovers can make the difference between separated low-wage workers or other low-balance participants remaining in plans or being forced out and then possibly transferred into forced-transfer IRAs.

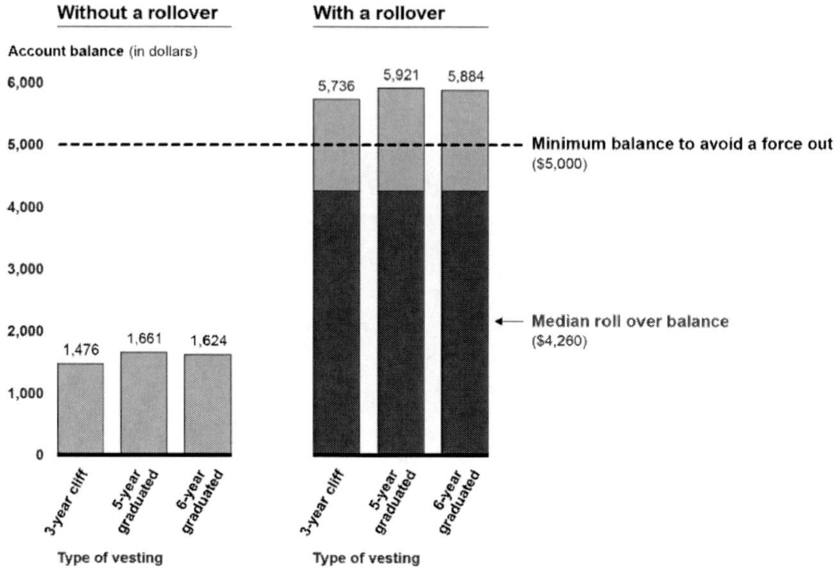

Source: GAO analysis of industry data regarding 401(k) plans' use of different plan rules and projections; Rollover data from ICI's report "The IRA Investor Profile: Traditional IRA Investors' Rollover Activity, 2007 and 2008". | GAO-15-73.

Notes: The projections assume the annual mean wage in 2013 ($21,580) for the service sector occupation with the most workers, specifically "food preparation and serving related occupations", including an annual raise of 2.36 percent, which is the average annual increase in wage over 15 years (1999-2013). For these assumptions, we referred to the U.S. Bureau of Labor Statistics' (BLS) Occupational Employment Statistics, Employment and Wage Estimates. We assumed a 2.2 year tenure, which is the 2014 median tenure for employed workers in the food preparation and serving related occupations, according to BLS data. We also assumed that employer contributions, when there were any, were made concurrently with employee contributions. More than half of defined contribution plans (such as 401(k) plans) are in the service sector and about 40 percent of defined contribution plan participants work in the service sector, according to 2011 data published by the Employee Benefits Security Administration. These projected amounts also reflect a 6.3 percent investment return, which is the geometric mean of 10-year returns for all target date funds according to our analysis of data from Morningstar.com. Target date funds are the most popular default investment for individuals automatically enrolled into 401(k) plans, according to the Plan Sponsor Council of America's (PSCA) *55th Annual Survey of Profit Sharing and 401(k) Plans*, which reflects the 2011 plan experience. The median rollover balance is for participants age 30-34 with an average income less than $35,000 in 2007, according to the Investment Company Institute. The

Investment Company Institute, *The IRA Investor Profile: Traditional IRA Investors' Rollover Activity, 2007 and 2008* (2010).

This projection reflects our 'moderate' assumptions for a low-wage worker's vested balances, which assumes a 3 percent employee contribution, a 50 percent employer match, and a 3-month service requirement. About 54 percent of plans that automatically enroll employees in the plan set a default contribution of 3 percent of salary and 48 percent of plans offer a 50 percent match, according to data from the Plan Sponsor Council of America's (PSCA) *55th Annual Survey of Profit Sharing and 401(k) Plans*. According to the same source, 16.6 percent of plans reported a service requirement of three months. Our assumptions for vesting schedules follow:

- Under 3-year cliff vesting, the employer's contribution is 100 percent vested after 3 years of service.
- Under graduated vesting, the employer's contribution is partially vested after each year of service, depending on how long the graduated vesting period is. For example, in our projections, we used:
    - for a 5-year graduated vesting schedule: 0, 25, 50, 75, 100 percent at the ends of years 1 through 5; and
    - for a 6-year gradated vesting schedule: 0, 20, 40, 60, 80, and 100 percent at the end of years 1 through 6.

Figure 4. Disregarding Rollover Balances Can Result in Low-Wage Workers' Vested Balances Falling Below the $5,000 Cap on Forced Transfers.

If the $19,500 balance used as an example in figure 3, which included rollover funds, had been left in a 401(k) plan and invested in a target date fund earning 6.3 percent, it would have gained more than $80,000 over 30 years, reflecting more than 400 percent growth, potentially much more than if it was invested conservatively in a forced-transfer IRA (see fig. 5).

Participants trying to consolidate their savings as they move from job to job could ultimately lose their ability to remain in a 401(k) plan with its choice of investments and could realize a lower retirement savings balance because of the current provision allowing rollover balances to be forcibly transferred out of the plan environment. Absent a change in law, active plans can continue to force out participants who have account balances over $5,000 by excluding rollover funds when calculating the vested balance, creating a disadvantage for those workers who change jobs and consolidate to keep their retirement savings in the plan environment. As we previously reported, investing in a workplace plan offers certain features that may suit individuals.[41]

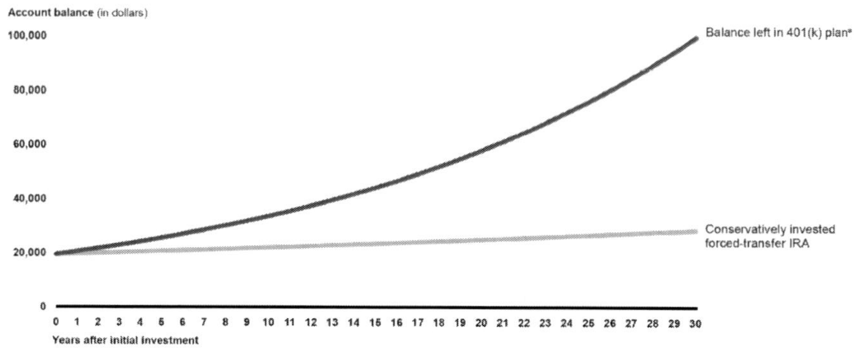

Source: GAO projection based on analysis of forced-transfer IRA and 401(k) industry data. | GAO-15-73.

Notes: We use a $19,500 balance for this example because it reflects the 401(k) balance workers might have if they rolled over their vested balances from prior employers several times ($5,000 x 3 jobs), but had less than a $5,000 vested balance (say $4,500) at their current plan. We used a target date fund investment for the plan projection because target date funds are the most popular default investment for 401(k) plans using automatic enrollment, according to Plan Sponsor Council of America's (55th) Annual Survey of Profit Sharing and 401(k) Plans. The 6.30 percent target date fund return is the geometric mean for the 10-year average returns through July 31, 2014, on all target date funds, which reflects our analysis of data from Morningstar.com. We assumed an 'all-in' 401(k) plan fee of .67 percent, which was the median participant and asset weighted all-in fee among defined contribution plans, according to an Investment Company Institute and Deloitte survey and report "Inside the Structure of Defined Contribution/401(k) Plan Fees, 2013: A study assessing the mechanics of the 'all-in' fee," published August 2014, that surveyed defined contribution plans covering a range of plan assets and participant counts for plans with assets of $1 million or more. For the forced-transfer IRA, we calculated the median account opening fee ($6.75) and the median annual fee ($42). We used the mean 10-year return for taxable money market funds, as calculated by us with data from Morningstar.com. An alternate projection using the 15-year mean return ending July 31, 2014 on taxable money market funds, which is 1.89 percent, resulted in a balance of $32,510, still about a third of what could be earned in a target date fund.

[a] "Balance left in 401(k) plan" projection assumes investment in a target date fund earning 6.30 percent with a 0.67 percent all-in fee. See general notes below for detail on these assumptions.

Figure 5. Projected Growth of $19,500 Balance Invested in a Forced-Transfer IRA or Left in a 401(k) Plan.

Low-Wage Workers' and Young Workers' Vested Balances May Often Fall Below the Required $5,000 Vested Balance Needed to Prevent Forced Transfers

Low-wage workers and young workers are vulnerable to forced transfers since they may change jobs often, which can leave them with particularly low balances. As shown in figure 3, we projected the vested balance of an average low-wage worker who: 1) earns $21,580 (the mean annual salary in 2013 for the largest occupational group within the service sector),[42] 2) works an average service sector tenure of 2.2 years, and 3) receives a 2.36 percent annual salary increase (the average annual change in earnings over 15 years from 1999 to 2013). We found that the vested balance fell below $5,000 even when using our "optimistic" assumptions.[43] (See appendix IV for more detail on the projections.) However, as discussed above, if the participant had transferred a small balance in a prior plan to their current plan, it could be enough to push their vested balance over the $5,000 cap, preventing a forced transfer, if plans were not permitted under current law to disregard rollover balances.

A service requirement [44]—the length of time a plan may require that someone work before participating in the 401(k) plan—like a vesting schedule, makes it harder for a worker to build up a vested balance that will exceed the $5,000 cap on forced transfers. In 2011, about 40 percent of plans used a service requirement.[45] Service requirements can result in smaller balances because a participant has less time to contribute to their account. If a plan imposes a service requirement and a vesting requirement, young workers and low-wage workers may not be able to accumulate vested balances over $5,000. As shown in table 3, the median tenure for workers age 20-24 is just 1.3 years.[46]

Table 3. Median Years of Tenure with Current Employer, by Age (January 2014)

Age	18-19	20-24	25-34	35 44	45-54	55-64	65+
Years of tenure	.8	1.3	3.0	5.2	7.9	10.4	10.3

Source: U.S. Bureau of Labor Statistics, Economic News Release, "Median years of tenure with current employer for employed wage and salary workers by age and sex, selected years, 2002-2014." This table shows the data for men and women combined. Release last modified Sept. 18, 2014. | GAO-15-73

KEEPING TRACK OF 401(K) PLAN ACCOUNTS CAN BE DIFFICULT BECAUSE OF CHALLENGES WITH CONSOLIDATION, COMMUNICATION, AND INFORMATION, BUT SSA IS IN A POSITION TO HELP

Having Multiple Accounts Makes It Difficult for Participants to Keep Track of Retirement Savings

401(k) plan participants often lose track of their accounts over time. In the United States, the responsibility is on the individual to manage their retirement savings, including keeping track of 401(k) plan accounts. The considerable mobility of U.S. workers increases the likelihood that many will participate in multiple 401(k) plans. Over the last 10 years, 25 million participants in workplace plans separated from an employer and left at least one account behind and millions left two or more behind.[47] When individuals hold multiple jobs, they may participate in many 401(k) plans or other types of employer-sponsored plans and upon changing jobs face recurring decisions about what to do with their plan savings. Figure 6 illustrates how a participant can accumulate multiple retirement accounts over a career.

Participants Face Challenges Consolidating 401(k) Plan Accounts

There are many reasons participants have multiple accounts for retirement savings. Currently, there is no standard way for participants to consolidate their accounts within the 401(k) plan environment. For example, employers do not always permit rollovers into their 401(k) plans. As we previously reported, there are barriers to plan-to-plan rollovers that DOL and IRS need to address to facilitate such rollovers when participants may wish to choose that option.[48] Absent plan-to-plan rollovers, participants frequently roll over their accounts into IRAs or leave their 401(k) savings with their former employers, both of which increase the number of accounts for the participants if they then go on to enroll in their new employers' plans. Plan-to-plan rollovers help reduce the number of lost accounts because the accounts stay with the participants. This option is, however, irrelevant if the new employer does not offer a plan.

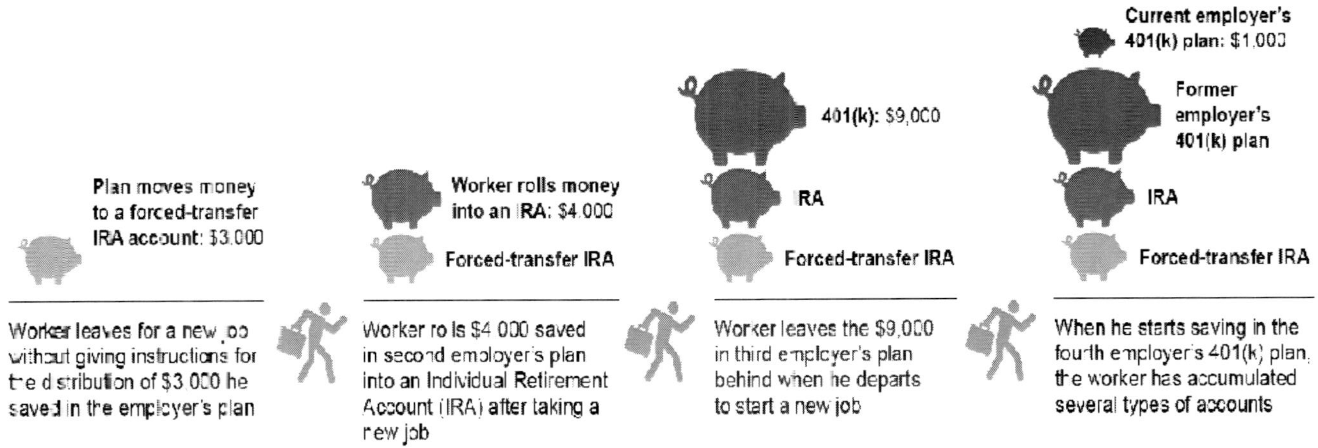

Source: GAO review of select laws and regulations. | GAO-15-73.

Figure 6. A Worker's Accumulation of Multiple Accounts for Retirement Savings.

Industry representatives we interviewed said automatic enrollment also contributes to participants having multiple accounts. Although automatic enrollment facilitates retirement saving, individuals may be less apt to pay attention to an account that they did not make the decision to enroll in. Industry professionals told us that individuals with a collection of many small accounts may forget about them because the small balances provide them less incentive to pay attention to them. In addition, automatic enrollment is likely to exacerbate the accumulation of multiple, small accounts. As more participants are brought into the system there could be an increase in forgotten accounts, because many of those participants are unengaged from the start, in spite of DOL notification requirements.[49] However, as GAO has previously reported automatic enrollment can significantly increase participation in 401(k) plans.[50]

Participants Face Challenges Communicating with Former Employers' Plans

When participants leave their savings in a plan after leaving a job, the onus is on them to update former employers with address and name changes, and to respond to their former plan sponsor's communications. Plans and record keepers have no automatic way to keep this information up to date for participants, nor do they have ways to ensure that separated participants will respond to their communications. For example, one industry professional noted that if former participants' e-mail contacts are work e-mails, they will lose contact with their plans when they change jobs and do not provide alternate e-mail addresses. When a plan loses track of a participant it can create a number of challenges because the plan has to spend time and incur the cost of searching for the participant. In addition, there are no standard practices among plans and providers for the frequency or method of conducting searches for missing or nonresponsive participants.

While there is agency guidance on searching for missing participants in terminating plans prior to forcing them out,[51] in hearings before the ERISA Advisory Council and in our interviews, providers and other industry professionals reported that the guidance on searches is unclear and insufficient. For instance, it is unclear how to satisfy disclosure requirements when the participant's address on file is known to be incorrect. One provider told us plans are obligated to make a "good faith effort" to locate participants, but they do not always know what a good faith effort entails. This leaves plans unsure of what steps they must take to satisfy applicable search requirements.

Participants Face Challenges Obtaining Information Useful for Keeping Track of 401(k) Plan Accounts

Employer actions, such as terminations, mergers, and bankruptcies can also make it difficult for participants to keep track of their accounts. Participants and beneficiaries can lose track of former employers' plans when the employers change location or name, merge with another company, spin-off a division of the company, or go out of business. DOL officials said that one of the most challenging problems facing participants and their advocates is tracking down lost plans. For example, company records for legacy plans, old plans that no longer have operating units, may be scattered, making employee and participant data difficult to locate, and the former plan's administrative staff may no longer be available to respond to questions regarding participant records.

The current regulatory environment also presents challenges to participants. Participants separating from their employer are to receive information about their accounts via multiple disclosures. Depending on the actions participants take regarding their accounts upon separation, their former employers will provide them and regulatory agencies with relevant required disclosures and reports. (See appendix VI for a list of selected disclosures required when participants separate from employment or when plans undergo certain types of corporate restructuring.) As participants change jobs over time and accumulate multiple accounts, those who remain engaged with their accounts will acquire a large volume of documentation. For example, the hypothetical worker from figure 6 who had separated from three jobs would receive at least nine different notices from the three plan sponsors. In the instances where the worker's 401(k) plan savings were transferred to another account, the worker would have been provided information about the new account. Over time, the worker would continue to receive annual—or sometimes quarterly—statements from each account as well as various other notices and disclosures depending on any changes in the structure or terms of the plans or accounts. Over 10 years, if that worker had no further job changes or changes to the existing accounts, routine account statements alone would result in at least 40 separate documents. If even one of the accounts issued quarterly statements, the number of documents would increase to 70, which does not include any disclosures the worker might receive about the underlying investments of the accounts or information regarding changes to a plan or IRA.

Participants may also have difficulty understanding the complex notices or account statements they receive. As we have previously reported, the quantity of information participants receive may diminish the positive effects such important information could have for them.[52] Our previous work found that participant disclosures do not always communicate effectively, participants often find the content overwhelming and confusing, and many participants rarely read the disclosures they receive.[53]

In addition, although 401(k) plans are required to report annually on plan design, finances, and other topics to DOL, IRS, and PBGC via the Form 5500 Series [54] and a number of other forms required by the IRS,[55] the information reported may not always result in a clear record or trail of employer or plan changes. For instance, DOL officials told us that many small plans fail to file an updated or final Form 5500, which would include a valuable piece of information, an employer identification number, which can be used to track a new plan resulting from a merger.[56] In the event of a plan termination, the plan administrator may file Form 5310, a request for a determination letter on a plan's qualified status, with the IRS, but must provide participants an "Notice to Interested Parties" notifying them of their right to comment on the plan termination. In certain instances of a company spinoff, only the plan that was in existence before the spinoff is required to file a Form 5310-A, making it difficult to trace the new plan back to the original plan. We recently reported that this notice confuses participants and it is difficult for the average pension plan participant to exercise their right to comment.[57] In addition, participants may receive a Notice of Plan Termination that includes information on their account balance, distribution options, and information about making an election and providing instructions to the plan.

Federal agency officials told us that inactive participants can fail to find their accounts with former employers and do not always know where to go to seek assistance or find information about their accounts. (See table 4 for descriptions of the role of federal agencies and other entities in helping participants find their plan accounts). Even with the information participants received while still active in plans or at separation, they then have to figure out which agencies and private sector entities to contact to find their accounts. Former employers and record keepers have information participants may need, but participants will need to have stayed in contact with their former employers to get that information. Federal agencies may also have some of the information that participants may need. However, the information that agencies provide is not designed to help participants keep track of multiple accounts or to find lost accounts. Consequently, participants searching for their accounts from former employers may have incomplete information. Moreover, if participants kept the notices and statements sent to them, the information they need may be out of date and located in multiple documents. As a result of such information challenges, even those who obtain assistance from benefits advisors with government or non-profit programs may be unable to locate all of their retirement savings.

Table 4. Federal Agencies or Entities That Can Help Former Participants Locate 401(k) Accounts

DOL's Office of Outreach, Education, and Assistance (OEA)	OEA is charged with assisting the public locate information about their retirement benefits from employers. OEA has direct contact with participants through benefits advisors that field calls to answer questions related to retirement savings. To assist the public, benefits advisors determine whether a participant's former employer is still in existence, and whether it has a new address. OEA conducts a search to determine when the employer may have filed an IRS Form 5500, looks for fiduciaries or service providers, uses an internal database to track changes recorded from previous calls, and references an informal list of mergers and acquisitions that has been developed to help reconnect individuals with their benefits. In some instances, OEA will contact a plan to see if benefits have been paid out and they encourage participants to check their own records for IRS 1099 forms that would signify a benefit distribution. OEA benefits advisors respond to requests for assistance, so participants have to know to reach out to DOL for assistance. DOL officials told us that about 60 percent of the benefit inquiries they receive originate from individuals who had received a notice of Potential Private Retirement Benefit Information—signifying retirement savings left behind in a plan—from SSA. DOL officials told us they helped 2,800 people to reclaim about $130 million in retirement savings. But industry professionals estimate there could be billions more in forced-transfer IRAs and uncashed plan distribution checks.
Pension Benefit Guaranty Corporation (PBGC)	PBGC offers a publication titled *Finding a Lost Pension* to help participants, and suggests documents participants may need while searching as well as sources of information and assistance, including other federal agencies and federally funded pension assistance centers. Some of the information that the publication says participants may need comes from the plan that the participant is trying to find. The publication acknowledges that it is hard to tell which source will provide participants with the information they need, that there are no guarantees of success, and that experienced pension counselors sometimes cannot find a lost pension. The publication suggests a search include: (1) trying to find the plan sponsor on the internet, (2) searching bankruptcy court filings if the employer went bankrupt, (3) asking former co-workers what happened to the company, (4) contacting any unions representing workers there, and (5) contacting the Chamber of Commerce in the town where the company was located. The publication suggests participants may be able to research corporate merger or buyout information at a specialized business library, contact one of the corporate officers listed in annual reports corporations submitted to state governments, or contact the plan's accountant, actuary, trustee, or attorney listed on the plan's annual report.

Table 4. (Continued)

Health and Human Services' Administration on Aging	The Administration on Aging assists individuals with issues related to their retirement security and funds non-profit pension counseling programs operated by organizations such as the Pension Rights Center and the Pension Action Center. At these centers, counselors assist callers find their pension benefits, often conducting searches for employers that are difficult to find due to bankruptcy or business restructuring. In some cases, benefit advisors cannot locate plans due to plans' changes in name, location, or other identifying information. One federally subsidized consumer advocacy group we interviewed helps about 200 people each year to find lost accounts. A representative of the organization said they serve only a small number of those who need help because many people are unaware of their services.

Source: GAO review of agency information and interviews with agency personnel. | GAO-15-73

SSA Can Help Participants Locate Accounts by Providing Information Earlier

The Social Security Administration (SSA) provides information that can help participants locate retirement savings left with a former employer. The Potential Private Retirement Benefit Information (Notice) includes information that could be beneficial to individuals looking for missing accounts, including: the name of the plan where a participant may have savings, the plan administrator's name and address, the participant's savings balance,[58] and the year that the plan reported savings left behind (see figure 7).

SSA sends the Notice when an individual files for Social Security benefits, which can occur as early as age 62, unless the notice is requested earlier.[59] Individuals appear to be generally unaware that this personal financial information exists or that they may request it from SSA, since few individuals request the form prior to retirement. SSA officials said that they only received about 760 requests for the form in 2013, though according to data provided by SSA the agency has records of potential benefits for over 33 million people. Agency officials told us that they were not aware of any potential advertising or effort on the agency's website (www.ssa.gov) for promoting the availability of the Notices or informing people about their ability to request the notices.[60] Officials also said that approximately 70,000 Notices are generated for new Social Security beneficiaries every month.

If You Want to Apply for These Benefits

If you want to apply for these retirement benefits or have any questions, you should contact the Plan Administrator shown below. The Plan Administrator provided the information as of the date in the "Year Reported" field below. If you or the worker has already filed a claim and received payment from the plan below, you may not be eligible for any additional benefits. Include a copy of this notice when you contact the Plan Administrator.

Plan Name	Plan Number	
	Identification Number	
	Year Reported	Estimated Amount
Plan Administrator and Address	Type of Benefit	Payment Frequency
	Units or Shares	Value of Account

IMPORTANT: See the other side of this page for an explanation of this information.

Source: GAO selected portion of Potential Private Retirement Benefit Information, SSA-L88-C1, Social Security Administration. | GAO-15-73.

Figure 7. Contents of the Notice of Potential Private Retirement Benefit Information That Could Be Helpful to Individuals Looking for Missing Retirement Accounts.

Individuals may receive multiple Notices at retirement if they have left savings in more than one employer plan over their career. Although the same information is reported on each form and SSA houses the data for years, the data are not compiled for ease of use by the recipient or for efficiency and cost-savings by the agency. Agency officials explained that in the past people worked for one company for most of their lives and were more likely to have had a traditional defined benefit pension plan, and consequently the format of the Notice only allows for data from one employer. Because the Notice is not currently formatted to display consolidated data on potential benefits from multiple employers, information on benefits from each employer must be sent separately to the participant. Given that many individuals will change jobs often throughout their working life, they can therefore expect to receive several different Notices, adding to the number of disclosures, communications, and notices they are expected to review, understand, and consider in managing their retirement savings. Combining multiple Notices could simplify the process of managing multiple forms for people with more than one account and reduce the costs to SSA.

More widely known, SSA also sends individuals a Social Security Statement (Statement) that estimates Social Security retirement benefits—at different claiming ages, and displays a worker's earnings history.[61] SSA suspended the mailing of paper copies of the Statement in 2011, but in 2014 resumed mailing the Statements to individuals every 5 years, starting at age 25.[62] This information is also available online to anyone who establishes an account. Similar to the Notice, the Statement contains important information about an individual's potential retirement income. Together these documents give individuals a more complete understanding of their income in retirement. SSA also has earnings recorded by employer, which is available upon request, but it is not mailed to individuals or available online. The earnings record for each year could provide clues as to when certain periods of employment occurred, which is key information that industry professionals suggest individuals looking for their lost 401(k) plan accounts should have when conducting a search. Given the multiple Notices individuals can receive from SSA, in addition to the Statement, finding a way to reduce duplication can help individuals keep track of their accounts and locate missing accounts. SSA has a process in place to review and revise the Statement and the agency already stores all of the data published in the Notice. As suggested in figure 8, providing the Notice at the same time as and with the Statement is one way to give individuals a consolidated, timely resource and reduce the volume of paperwork they need to keep track of over time.

As noted earlier, when plans lose track of participants due to outdated mailing addresses, participants fail to receive critical plan communications about their accounts and about any changes to the plan name or administrator that will be vital when they want to communicate with the plan and claim their benefits. An industry professional we interviewed suggested that participants receive some type of reminder to notify plans of address changes. If participants are reminded of their inactive 401(k) plan accounts via the Notice and prompted to inform plans of updated address information, the accounts may be less likely to become lost. Making the information available online or mailing it every 5 years can remind participants of the multiple accounts they have. Providing the combined information on inactive accounts from multiple employers can also give individuals needed information to keep track of their multiple accounts and provide the opportunity to correct inaccurate account information. In addition, having a reminder of the accounts they left behind may increase the likelihood that participants pay attention to other plan communications.

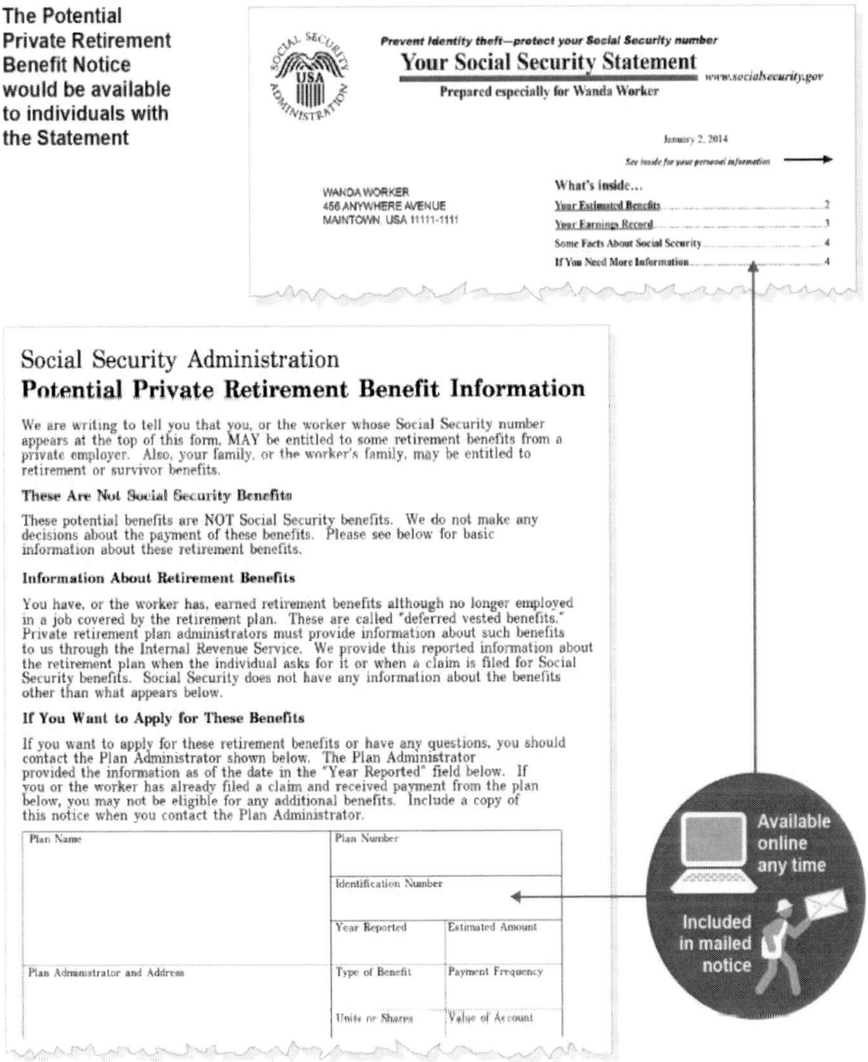

Source: Social Security Administration, Social Security Statement, Form SSA-7005-SM, and Potential Private Retirement Benefit Information, SSA-L99-C1 | GAO-15-73.

Figure 8. Consolidating Multiple Notices of Potential Private Retirement Benefit Information with the Social Security Statement Can Consolidate Information Critical to Individuals for Tracking Multiple Accounts.

OTHER COUNTRIES HAVE TAKEN ACTIONS TO PROTECT FORCED TRANSFERS AND TRACK RETIREMENT ACCOUNTS

To manage inactive workplace retirement accounts, officials in the countries in our study told us that the United Kingdom (U.K.), Switzerland, and Australia use forced transfers and Australia, Denmark, Belgium and the Netherlands use tracking tools. Like the forced-transfer IRAs of the United States, the forced transfers we were told about in these countries transfer account balances without participant consent. In the countries we studied with forced transfers, those accounts follow participants changing jobs, are efficiently managed in a single fund, or are free from fees at a government agency. Each of these approaches helps to preserve the real value of the account for the participant, and generally ensures workplace plans will not be left with the expenses of administering small, inactive retirement accounts. Although the models employed vary by country, the three countries with tracking tools we studied allow participants online access to consolidated information on their workplace retirement accounts, referred to as "pension registries" in this report. Approaches include both databases and "service bus" interfaces connecting providers to participants in real time.[63] Roles for government in these countries range from holding the data and analyzing it for tax and social policy purposes to collaborating with an industry-created pension registry, allowing for information on national pension benefits to be provided in the registry.

Forced Transfers in Other Countries Benefit Participants

According to officials we interviewed in the three countries that use forced transfers, they have legislation that (1) consolidates transferred accounts, either in a participant's new plan or with other forcibly-transferred accounts, and (2) enables these accounts to grow, either at a rate comparable to participants' current retirement accounts or at least in pace with inflation (see table 5).

Table 5. Characteristics of Forced Transfers in Three Countries and in the United States

	United Kingdom	Switzerland	Australia	United States
When was legislation enacted?	2014	1993	2012a	2001
Under what circumstances are accounts forcibly transferred?	When an employee's new plan identifies an eligible balance	When they have been inactive between 6 and 24 monthsb	12 months of inactivity	Plans meeting legal requirements may transfer eligible balances at their discretion and at plan termination.
What is the maximum account size that can be forcibly transferred?	£10,000 (about $17,000)c	Any amount	AUD 2,000 (currently about $1,860)d	$5,000e
Where are forced transfers sent?	Consolidated into the employee's current planf	Consolidated into a single fundg	Consolidated at the Australian Tax Office	Used to open a forced-transfer IRA
Over time, what happens to forced-transfer balances?	Balances grow according to returns on investments in the employee's current plan	Balances grow according to returns on central fund investments, which are similar to returns in workplace plans	Balances keep pace with inflation	Balances often decrease

Source: GAO analysis of documents discussing retirement policies in these countries and interviews with government officials. | GAO-15-73.

[a] A 2009 law required accounts under AUD 200 to be transferred after 5 years of inactivity. In 2012, that legislation was amended to reflect the content shown here.

[b] Plans must allow participants 6 months to initiate a transfer to a new plan or an individual account or policy with a bank or insurer. While plans can forcibly transfer participants after 6 months, they must forcibly transfer participants after 24.

[c] In the United Kingdom, regulations implementing the forced-transfer law have not yet been finalized. However, the U.K. Department for Work and Pensions has tested different account sizes and determined the size of account it plans to include.

[d] 2014 legislation contemplates further raising the accounts size eligible for forced transfer to AUD 4,000 at the end of 2015 and AUD 6,000 at the end of 2016.

[e] While $5,000 is the cap on forced transfers of new vested plan balances, because the law permits plans to disregard rollovers and their earnings from previous plans when calculating the vested balances, in the absence of any participant instructions, much larger balances can be transferred.

There is no limit on the size of a participant balance that may be transferred to a forced-transfer IRA by a terminating plan.

[f] U.K. employers must choose a plan for their employees working in the United Kingdom under a 2008 U.K. law. To ensure employers have an easy, low-cost option available, that law created the National Employment Savings Trust, a non-profit, workplace plan available to any employer in the United Kingdom. Mandatory automatic enrollment began in 2012 and will include all employers beginning in 2018.

[g] The Swiss Substitute Occupational Benefits Institution (Substitute Plan) also serves as a means for employers who do not offer their own plan but are required to provide their employees retirement benefits to do so, and for the self-employed to participate in a retirement plan if they wish.

Switzerland—According to Swiss officials, forced transfers in Switzerland are consolidated in a single fund, the Substitute Plan, administered by a non-profit foundation and invested until claimed by participants (see fig. 9). The Substitute Plan serves as a back-up in those instances when participants fail to roll their money over to their new plan, as they are required to do by law, according to Swiss Federal Social Insurance Office officials.

Plans report information on inactive accounts to the Guarantee Fund, the Swiss organization insuring insolvent workplace plans. After 2 years of inactivity, those accounts must be transferred to the Substitute Plan. Officials said the Guarantee Fund is responsible for returning the retirement savings of participants to them in retirement.[64] According to officials at the Swiss Federal Social Insurance Office, the Substitute Plan held about $5.5 to $6.6 billion in 2014. They said its investments have outperformed those in workplace plans in recent years, and compared to most workplace plans, its administrative costs are low, in part because the board manages the investments itself. According to a Substitute Plan board member, the board receives investment guidance from financial experts who counsel its investment committee.

The United Kingdom—Officials said that the United Kingdom "pot-follows-member" law is designed to make workplace retirement accounts move with participants throughout their career, or at least until the balances are large enough that they could be used to buy an annuity.[65]

Transfers of participants' savings from a former employer are initiated by the new employer when it is notified, likely through information technology, of an eligible account.[66]

Although every employer in the United Kingdom must automatically enroll workers between age 22 and retirement age who earn more than about $17,000 a year, U.K. officials are still considering how they will implement the law when no new plan exists to transfer money to. They said one benefit of putting the responsibility on the new plan is that the trigger for the transfer does not occur until a new plan exists.

Once implemented, the pot-follows-member law will automate the plan-to-plan rollover process for participants, keep transferred assets under participant direction, and generally ensure plans do not manage small, inactive accounts.

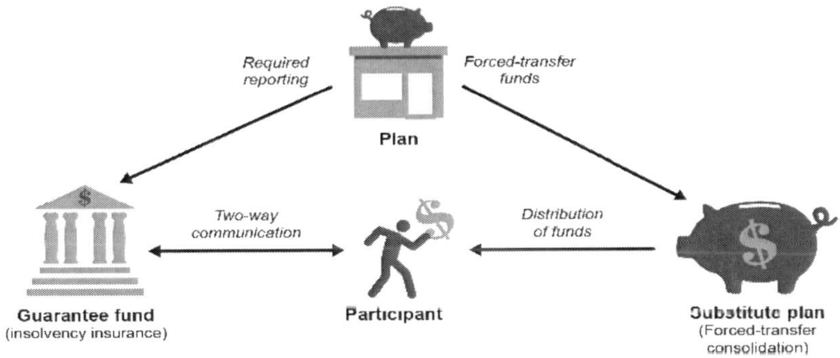

Source: GAO analysis of documents describing Swiss transfer policy and statements from Swiss officials. | GAO-15-73.

Note: The Swiss use a foundation entrusted by law with special tasks, the Substitute Occupational Benefits Institution (Substitute Plan) to hold accounts in workplace plans that were inactive and thus transferred. Plans report information on inactive accounts to the Guarantee Fund, the Swiss organization insuring insolvent workplace plans, and send accounts within two years of inactivity to the Substitute Plan. The Guarantee Fund notifies participants of any accounts they have in the Substitute Plan when they retire, and upon request.

Figure 9. Inactive Retirement Accounts in Switzerland Are Invested in a Central Fund.

Figure 10 depicts three ways workplace retirement accounts can follow job-changing participants.[67]

Australia—Rather than invest forcibly transferred accounts for long-term growth, officials told us the Australian government preserves value while taking proactive steps to reconnect participants with their accounts. Accounts inactive for 1 year are transferred to the Australian Tax Office (ATO), which holds them in a no-fee-environment and pays returns equal to inflation when they are claimed.[68]

When participants access the ATO website to submit their taxes or change their address, they are provided a link to view any account they have that is held by the ATO, and they can consolidate it with another account online. Unlike the United Kingdom and Switzerland, the Australian approach requires participants to take action to invest their transferred accounts for long-term growth, although it provides a tool to help them do so.

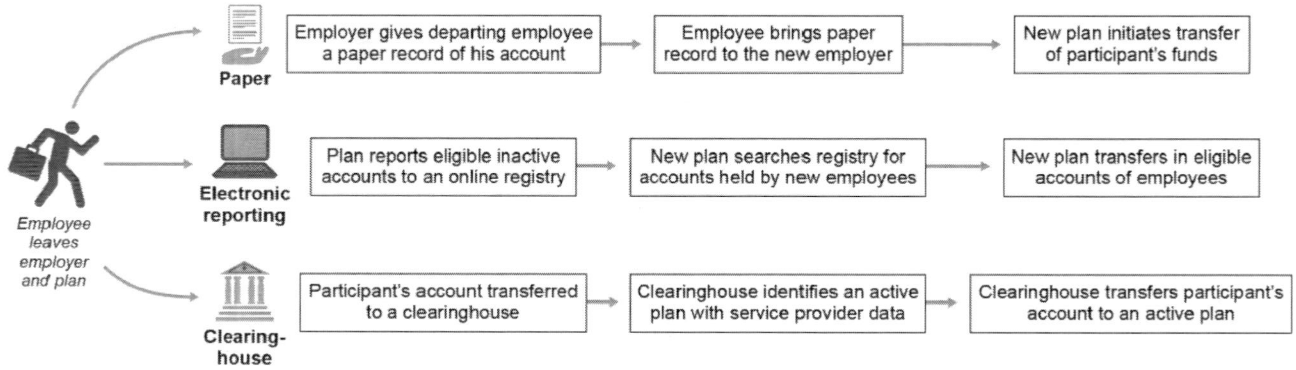

Source: GAO interviews with relevant officials and account transfer policy documents. | GAO-15-73.

Note: Swiss plan participants are required by law to pass a paper record of their workplace retirement account information to their new employer, and ensure it happens in most circumstances by requiring them to do so by law. One solution contemplated by 2014 legislation in the United Kingdom is a database of inactive accounts eligible for transfer to a new employer which a new employer can use to initiate a transfer. The clearinghouse method is one beginning to be used in the United States, where service provider data allows a clearinghouse to find a participant's account in their active 401(k) plan and transfer an account that was forcibly transferred from a prior plan into their new one.

Figure 10. Three Possible Ways Workplace Retirement Accounts Can Follow Job-Changing Participants.

Other Countries Provide Pension Registries to Help Participants Track Accounts while the United States Does Not Have a Similar Approach

European Commission officials we talked to said that the most basic form of centralized information on plans should help participants find providers, allow them to view which plans serve which employers, and provide relevant plan contact information. All of the approaches we reviewed in the selected countries went further. The Netherlands, Australia, and Denmark provide consolidated, online information—called pension registries—to participants on all of their workplace retirement accounts, and Belgium is scheduled to do the same by 2016. The pension registry designs in the four countries we studied with such registries share some common elements that make them useful for participants.

- *Active and inactive accounts:* All include data on both active and inactive accounts, including account balances and plan or insurer contact information.
- *Website accessibility:* All include the identity authentication necessary to securely allow online access to individual participants.
- *Workplace account information:* All include information on workplace retirement accounts.

While various benefits to participants were cited as the impetus for creating registries in each of these countries, pension registries can be used by plans as well. A representative of one workplace plan in Belgium said they use pension registry data to find missing participants, make payments to the participant as planned, and eliminate liabilities for those payments.[69] The representative also added that when the pension registry goes live to participants the plan may spend less time answering questions from participants who do not have a clear understanding of their rights to benefits. Instead, they will refer participants to the pension registry for answers.[70] Plans in Australia also use the pension registry to identify inactive accounts their participants have in other plans and to talk to participants about consolidating their accounts. Table 6 shows various attributes of the pension registries in the countries we included in our study. Further details on these pension registries can be found in appendix VII.

Table 6. Attributes of Pension Registries Used in Four Countries in 2014

	Denmark	The Netherlands	Belgium	Australia
Does it include broad information to facilitate retirement planning?	Yes	Planned	No	No
Does it include information on national, workplace, and personal retirement income sources?	All	Workplace and national	Workplace and nationala	Workplace only
How is it financed?	By pension providers voluntarily	Per-participant fee paid by pension providers	Government general revenue	Government general revenue and pension industry tax
What was the impetus for the creation of the registry?	To help individuals track multiple accounts, locate lost ones, and plan for retirement	To help individuals track multiple accounts, locate lost ones and plan for retirementb	To give government information for tax and social policy purposes and find lost accounts.	To help individuals track multiple accountsand locate lost ones, and encourage consolidation

Source: GAO analysis of documentation of pension registries in other countries and interviews with government officials and other stakeholders in the listed countries. | GAO-15-73.

[a] A representative of one Belgian plan said information on national retirement benefits (equivalent to Social Security in the United States) are planned to be incorporated into Belgium's pension registry in 2016.

[b] Representatives of the Dutch industry association said their pension registry can give participants a clearer understanding of their finances in retirement, and helps manage their expectations. They said many Dutch citizens believe their pension income will be 70 percent of their working income, when it will actually be just 40 or 50 percent.

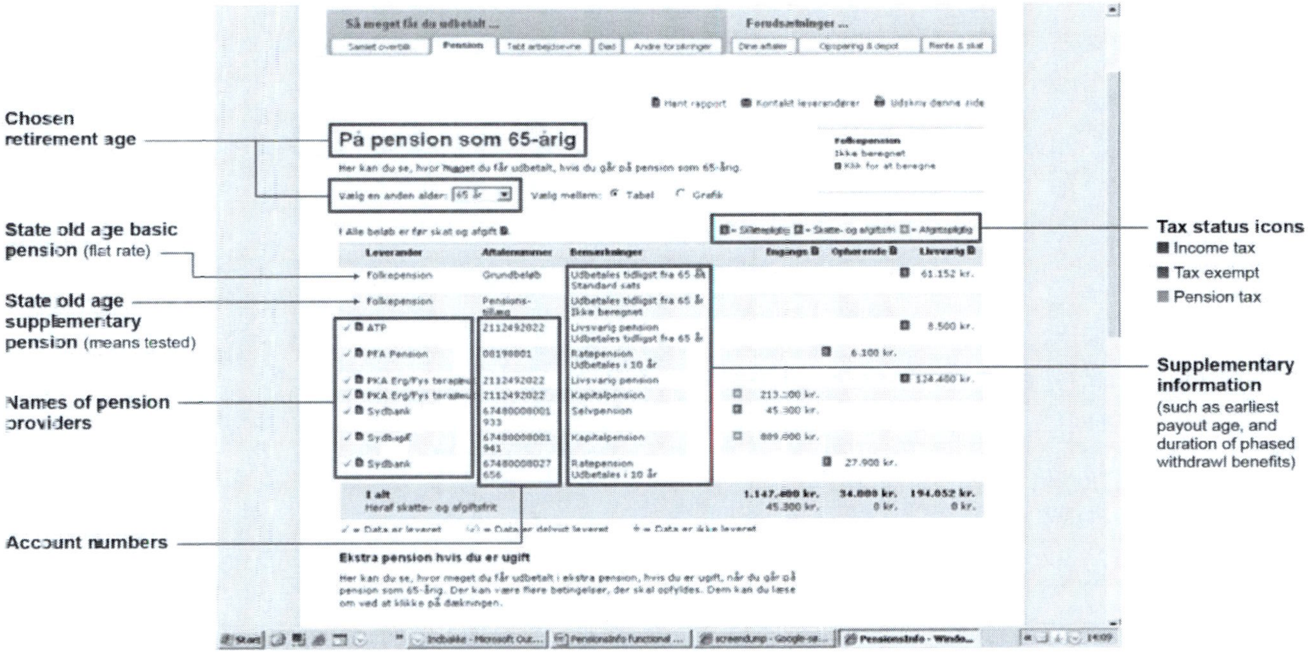

Source: GAO analysis of the Danish Pension Registry Pensionsinfo, https://www.pensionsinfo.dk. | GAO-15-73.

Note: The Danish pension registry provides Danes with current, consolidated, retirement account information on their workplace plans, individual plans, and government retirement benefits online. This screenshot shows some of the information accessible to participants.

Figure 11. Danish Pension Registry Screenshot.

Denmark—Denmark's pension registry incorporates personal retirement accounts similar to IRAs in the United States, and facilitates retirement planning by allowing participants to see how their financial security in retirement varies with factors like retirement age and spend-down option, according to documentation provided by Danish officials.[71] Although the Danish pension registry is a private non-profit organization financed by participating pension providers, it also works with the government to provide data on public retirement benefits (see fig. 11).[72]

The Netherlands—Participants have had access to the pension registry since 2011 using a national digital ID, following the enactment of legislation in 2006 and 2008. The Dutch Social Insurance Bank worked for years with the largest pension plans to develop the registry, though the pension industry in general—including insurance companies and smaller pension funds—provided input into the registry, according to industry representatives we interviewed. The pension industry's web portal collects and consolidates pension information from funds and insurers when a participant logs in to the system. Participants can also access national, or government, pension information. The pension registry does not store the information in a central location because of security concerns over participants' private information, according to representatives of the pension registry we interviewed. The government plans to expand the pension registry into a pension dashboard that will project retirement benefits under various life events and allow participants to view their entire financial situation to facilitate retirement planning. The aim of the expansion is to increase financial literacy but also affect behavior.

Australia—Participants can access the pension registry, the SuperSeeker, online using a unique electronic government ID. Participants can also use a phone service or smart phone application to get the information, according to the SuperSeeker website. With SuperSeeker, participants can view all of their workplace retirement accounts on the web, including active and inactive accounts, and any lost accounts held by ATO. SuperSeeker can also be used to locate lost accounts not held by ATO. The content of the registry is generated by plans, as they are required to report the details of all lost accounts twice each year to the ATO, in addition to active accounts.

Belgium—Officials told us individual participant access is planned for 2016 using a national digital signature. They said the law creating the workplace pension registry was passed in 2006. Pension providers are required by law to submit workplace pension information to the registry. An electronic database of national pensions (similar to Social Security in the United States) already existed for private sector workers and in 2011, the government included public sector workers in the database to create a unified national and workplace pension registry. Starting in 2016, all participants will be able to securely access the integrated data on both national and workplace retirement plans, according to Belgian government officials.

The European Commission Is Developing a Pan-European Pension Registry

European Commission officials told us Denmark has the most advanced pension registry and, as such, is a model for an international registry accessible by participants across the European Union. With a population of over 500 million in 28 member states, the European Union is more similar to the United States in terms of population and geographic size than the individual countries we included in our study, thus the challenges the European Union faces in setting up a pension registry may be particularly relevant for the United States. By creating a pan-European pension registry, European Commission officials said they aim to ensure that workers moving across borders do not lose portions of their retirement entitlements accrued in different jobs and countries. According to European Union data, more European workers are internationally mobile in the labor market, with the number of economically active European Union citizens working across borders having increased from 5 million in 2005 to 8 million in 2013. Their accumulated retirement benefits are scattered over several countries, making it difficult for participants to keep track of them, and for providers to locate missing participants.

Because some countries in Europe already have pension registries, European Commission officials said a European registry may involve linking existing registries together.[73] To this end, the European Commission has hired a consortium of six experienced pension providers from the Netherlands, Denmark, and Finland to study possible approaches and come up with a pilot project on cross-border pension tracking. This Track and Trace Your Pension in Europe project presented its initial findings in support of a European Tracking Service to the European Commission. The track and trace project found no uniform approach to pension tracking in the European Union. Although 16 countries report having a national pension tracking service, according to track and trace project documentation, these vary substantially in terms of functionality, coverage, service level, and complexity.

The European Commission expects to face challenges implementing a pension registry in the European Union because tax laws and languages vary from country to country. European Commission officials said they face several challenges: the standardization required for all plans in all European Union countries to interface with the same system, the data security required for all those involved to trust the system, and questions about how the system would be financed. For example, according to the track and trace project's initial findings, few countries have a standardized format on pension communication, though most report having legal requirements for providers to inform participants on a regular basis. These differences across countries reflect the different levels of maturity of the pension systems across Europe. European Commission officials noted it is likely to take many years to standardize data. However, as representatives of the Dutch Association of Insurers pointed out, unless the trend of increasingly frequent job changes reverses, a pension registry will only become more important in the future.

The United States Lacks a Pension Registry That Can Provide New Opportunities for Participants

Currently, there is no national pension registry in the United States. No single agency or group of agencies have responsibility for developing a pension registry for participants looking for their accounts, and no coalition of financial firms in the retirement industry has acted alone in lieu of government involvement. While projects to provide access to current, consolidated information on workplace retirement accounts are complete or in the final stages in other countries, the United States has not undertaken a coordinated effort to determine how to provide the same to Americans. The current piecemeal approach involving the Department of Labor (DOL), the Pension Benefit Guaranty Corporation (PBGC), Health and Human Services (HHS), and the Social Security Administration (SSA) is largely reactive. Participants often turn to DOL, HHS, or PBGC for assistance once their accounts are lost, and SSA generally only provides information once participants have reached retirement age. The current approach also requires a high level of participant engagement with complex financial information. The current state of financial literacy in the United States and the field of behavioral economics suggest that this kind of participant engagement should not be expected. As discussed earlier, the task of tracking down retirement savings is a substantial challenge for participants who may lack information that would allow other entities to help them find accounts. Similarly, the inactive account information SSA provides pertains to "potential" benefits, leaving the participant to determine whether they exist or not.

The pension registries in the countries we reviewed are relatively proactive, and rely less on participant engagement. Their approach of providing access to current, consolidated information on all workplace retirement accounts may help prevent an account from being lost, and the need for a participant to work with government to find it. That approach also relies less on participants, as they need not keep records or update their address with plans to ensure they can later receive their benefits. For example, Australia was able to develop a registry that allows a participant to consolidate their benefits online on a single website, without engaging directly with either plan or calling a government funded assistance program.

Congress is aware of the problem participants have tracking accounts, and the Pension Protection Act of 2006 expanded PBGC's Missing Participant Program.[74] Two industry associations have also suggested that a central database be created that participants can check to determine whether they have a lost account in any ongoing plan in addition to any from terminated plans. Some of the groundwork for consolidating various pieces of information is already in place in the United States through large service providers that manage data on thousands of plans and millions of account holders. For example, information on retirement savings in many IRAs, workplace plans, and Social Security is already accessed online. While the U.S. retirement system is different from those in the countries with pension registries we studied, and the appropriate scope, oversight, and financing method for a pension registry in the United States have not been determined, the variety of examples in place in the countries we reviewed provide ideas to consider. Currently, DOL and other federal agencies do not have any ongoing efforts to develop such a registry. Until there is a concerted effort to determine the potential for a U.S. pension registry, it may be premature to say whether U.S. workers can benefit from the same information as participants in some other countries.

CONCLUSION

The United States has a highly mobile labor force and an economy marked by frequent business formations and failures. The accessibility and portability of the U.S. account-based 401(k) plan system presumably allow participants to retain and manage their retirement assets throughout their careers, even with multiple job changes. However, there are some significant limitations with regard to portability and information access as a result of the current structure and rules of the 401(k) plan system. Given the expected continued growth of this system and the expansion of automatic enrollment, the number of inactive participants and inactive accounts—and the associated challenges—will almost certainly grow, exacerbating inefficiency and eroding the retirement security of U.S. workers.

Under current law, there is no mechanism in place that would allow plans or regulators to develop or consider additional default destinations when employees are forced out of 401(k) plans. Although other countries' approaches pose implementation challenges within the United States, there may be ways that DOL and Treasury, if given the authority to do so, can revise the current forced-transfer model to help achieve better financial outcomes for participants while still providing plans with administrative relief.

Another way to protect participants' 401(k) plan savings is by ensuring that all accounts with balances over $5,000 may remain in the plan environment, even when portions of those balances are from rollovers. Current law addresses the needs of plans and participants by alleviating the burden on plans of maintaining small, inactive accounts, while protecting participants with large balances from forced transfer. Changing the law so that active plans can no longer force-transfer accounts with balances over $5,000 by disregarding rollovers can extend current protections to all accounts of that size, while at the same time continuing to provide plans relief from maintaining small, inactive accounts. Regardless of the size of the balance that is transferred into a forced-transfer IRA, one way to partially mitigate the problems with these accounts is to broaden the investment options for these accounts from the limited conservative menu currently available. DOL can take steps to expand the menu of investment options available under its safe harbor regulations, to include alternatives similar to those available to automatically enrolled 401(k) plan participants. This would enable forced-transfer IRAs to be better protected from erosion by fees and inflation and provide better long-term outcomes for participants.

Workforce mobility and frequent changes in corporate structure can result in forgotten accounts, missing participants, and ultimately, lost retirement savings. Participants often have difficulty locating accounts in plans with former employers, especially those employers that have undergone some type of corporate restructuring. SSA holds critical information on accounts left in former employers' plans, but individuals rarely see that information before retirement and may be unaware that the information exists. As time passes, the information can become outdated and, therefore, less useful to participants trying to locate their retirement savings. Making this information easier to access and available sooner—such as by using the online system for Social Security earnings and benefit statements—can provide participants with a timelier reminder of accounts left in former employers' plans and provide them better opportunities for keeping track of accounts and improving their retirement security.

The lack of a simple way for participants to access information about their retirement accounts is a central problem of our current workplace retirement system. We found that other countries with robust private account-based retirement systems have been grappling with this challenge and have determined that pension registries can provide a meaningful long-term solution. Creating an accurate, easy to access, and easy to use pension registry in the United States would need to take into account important design challenges, including the scope of the data to be included, the entity that would oversee the registry, and how it would be financed. Designing a registry would also require serious discussions among the key stakeholders, including industry professionals, plan sponsor representatives, consumer representatives, and federal government stakeholders on what such a system should look like in the American context. However, the creation of a viable, effective registry in the United States could provide vital information regarding retirement security in a single location to millions of American workers.

Matters for Congressional Consideration

To better protect the retirement savings of individuals who change jobs, while retaining policies that provide 401(k) plans relief from maintaining small, inactive accounts, Congress should consider amending current law to:

1) Permit the Secretary of Labor and the Secretary of the Treasury to identify and designate alternative default destinations for forced transfers greater than $1,000, should they deem them more advantageous for participants.
2) Repeal the provision that allows plans to disregard amounts attributable to rollovers when determining if a participant's plan balance is small enough to forcibly transfer it.

Recommendations for Executive Action

To ensure that 401(k) plan participants have timely and adequate information to keep track of all their workplace retirement accounts, we recommend that the Social Security Administration's Acting Commissioner make information on potential vested plan benefits more accessible to individuals before retirement. For example, the agency could consolidate information on potential vested benefits, currently sent in the Potential Private Retirement Benefit Information notice, with the information provided in the Social Security earnings and benefits statement.

To prevent forced-transfer IRA balances from decreasing due to the low returns of the investment options currently permitted under the Department of Labor's safe harbor regulation, we recommend that the Secretary of Labor expand the investment alternatives available. For example, the forced-transfer IRA safe harbor regulations could be revised to include investment options currently under the qualified default investment alternatives regulation applicable to automatic enrollment, and permit forced-transfer IRA providers to change the investments for IRAs already established.

To ensure that individuals have access to consolidated online information about their multiple 401(k) plan accounts, we recommend that the Secretary of Labor convene a taskforce to consider establishing a national pension registry. The taskforce could include industry professionals, plan sponsor representatives, consumer representatives, and relevant federal government stakeholders, such as representatives from SSA, PBGC, and IRS, who could identify areas to be addressed through the regulatory process, as well as those that may require legislative action.

Agency Comments and Our Evaluation

We provided a draft of this report to the Department of Labor, the Social Security Administration, the Department of the Treasury, the Internal Revenue Service, the Pension Benefit Guaranty Corporation, the Securities and Exchange Commission, and the Consumer Financial Protection Bureau. DOL, SSA, Treasury and IRS, PBGC, and SEC provided technical comments, which we have incorporated where appropriate. DOL and SSA also provided formal comments. CFPB did not have any comments.

GAO Response to DOL Comments

DOL agreed to evaluate the possibility of convening a taskforce to consider the establishment of a national pension registry. We appreciate that

DOL shares our concerns and agrees that there is need for a comprehensive solution to problems related to missing and unresponsive participants. DOL stated, however, that it does not have the authority to establish or fund a registry. Specifically, DOL noted that it does not have authority to require reporting of the information needed for a registry or to arrange for the consolidation of retirement account information from multiple agencies. We reached the same conclusion and for that reason recommended a taskforce as a starting point for the development of a national pension registry. In fact, our recommendation noted that one role for the taskforce would be identifying areas that could be addressed through the regulatory process and those requiring legislative action. DOL also noted that an expansion of PBGC's missing participant program to include defined contribution plans could address some of these issues. It is our view that there may be a number of policies or programs that could address these problems and we agree that an expansion of PBGC's program could ultimately be part of a comprehensive solution. Should the taskforce determine that the most appropriate option or options require additional authority for DOL or other agencies, such options should be given careful congressional consideration.

DOL disagreed with our recommendation to expand the investment alternatives available under the safe harbor for plan sponsors using forced transfers. While DOL characterized our recommendation as calling for the safe harbor to include qualified default investment alternatives, our recommendation is to "expand the investment options available" and we noted that qualified default investment alternatives could be one option. DOL stated that the limited investments under the safe harbor are appropriate because Congress' intent for the safe harbor was to preserve principal transferred out of plans. Particularly, DOL noted that given the small balances and the inability of absent participants to monitor investments, the current conservative investment options are a more appropriate way to preserve principal.

However, as we show in the report on pages 9-13, the current forced-transfer IRA investment options like money market funds can protect principal from investment risk, but not from the risk that fees (no matter how reasonable) and inflation can result in decreased account balances due to returns on these small balance accounts not keeping pace with fees. Consequently, as our analysis shows and as several forced-transfer IRA providers told us, the reality has been that many forced-transfer IRAs have experienced very large and even complete declines in principal.

Regarding our analysis, DOL stated that the performance information that we used to illustrate the effects of low returns on forced-transfer IRAs on pages 9-13 and 20-21 covers too short a period and does not reflect the periodic higher returns earned by money market funds in the more distant past. Our projection in figure 2, p.13, showing the effect of returns from a money market investment versus a target date fund investment on a small balance over 30 years used 10-year mean returns for these investments. Given that the safe harbor for these accounts was issued 10 years ago in 2004, we feel a 10-year average is more appropriate and accurately reflects the returns earned. However, using a longer time period does not materially change our conclusions. A similar calculation using a 15-year mean return shows that these forced-transfer IRA accounts would still not be preserved. (See notes under fig. 2, p.13, and fig 5, p.20-21.)

In any case, our recommendation did not aim to eliminate money market funds from investments covered by the safe harbor but to expand the investment alternatives available so that plans and providers that want to operate under the safe harbor have the opportunity to choose the most suitable investment. We stand by our recommendation and encourage DOL to expand the safe harbor to include investment alternatives more likely to preserve principal and even increase it over time. Qualified default investment alternatives could be one option, although certainly not the only one, that could be considered.

GAO Response to SSA Comments

SSA disagreed with our recommendation to make information on potential private retirement benefits more accessible to individuals before retirement. SSA was concerned that our recommendation would place the agency in the position of having to respond to public queries about ERISA. SSA noted that the agency has no firsthand legal or operational knowledge of pension plans or the private pension system and should not be in a position of responding to questions of that nature or about ERISA, which it considered to be outside the scope of SSA's mission. We agree with SSA's view about providing information or advice about private pension plans generally. However, as SSA noted, the Notice of Potential Private Retirement Benefit Information (referred to as the "ERISA notice" in SSA's letter) already directs recipients to contact DOL with any questions. We would expect that any changes made to make information on potential vested plan benefits more accessible to individuals before retirement would continue to direct recipients to contact DOL with questions about ERISA policy.

SSA stated that it will seek legal guidance to determine if it is permissible to include a general statement encouraging potential beneficiaries to pursue any external pension benefits in its benefit Statement. As noted in our report on pages 30-31, individuals may be unaware of the availability of information on potential retirement benefits, therefore we support SSA's initiative to include language in the Statement encouraging potential beneficiaries to pursue external pension benefits. SSA also stated that there is no interface between potential private retirement information and Social Security benefits. However, as noted in our report on page 31, SSA already stores the potential vested benefits data and provides the information in the Statement. Consolidating the two types of information and making it available every 5 years can provide participants with timely and adequate information to keep track of all of their work place retirement accounts and could possibly lead to administrative efficiencies. Therefore, it may be appropriate for SSA to explore its concern about its legal authority to expend appropriated funds to disclose information that it already provides to the relevant beneficiary, on a more frequent basis and in a more consolidated manner. We continue to believe that this recommendation could enhance the retirement security of millions of Americans, who would benefit from the assistance in keeping track of their multiple accounts from multiple employers and becoming more knowledgeable about funds they may be due in retirement. Should SSA determine that they have authority to implement this legislation, we would strongly urge the agency's action. However, should SSA decide that it does not have the authority to move ahead on this recommendation, we would urge the agency to seek the necessary statutory authority.

Charles Jeszeck,
Director
Education, Workforce, and Income Security Issues

APPENDIX I: OBJECTIVES, SCOPE, AND METHODOLOGY

This report examines (1) what happens to forced-transfer individual retirement accounts (IRA) over time; (2) the challenges 401(k) plan participants face keeping track of their retirement savings and what, if anything, is being done to help them; and (3) how other countries address the challenges of inactive accounts.

To understand what happens to forced-transfer IRAs over time, as well as challenges 401(k) plan participants face keeping track of multiple 401(k) plan accounts, we reviewed relevant data from government, research, and industry sources. Because we found no comprehensive data on the number of IRA accounts opened as a result of forced transfers or other data relevant to their use and management, we collected data from a non-generalizeable group of 10 providers of forced-transfer IRAs about their practices and outcomes, including three of the largest IRA providers. There is no comprehensive list of all forced-transfer IRA providers. For this reason, we built a list of forced-transfer IRA providers through interviews with industry professionals, a review of IRA market data, and online searches. Our objective was to create a group that would cover a large share of assets in the forced-transfer IRA market and represent both small and large forced-transfer IRA providers in terms of company size. We reached out to the largest IRA providers by assets under management, as well as all small forced-transfer IRA providers on our list. We obtained forced-transfer IRA account data from 10 forced-transfer IRA providers that represent this mix of characteristics. We also interviewed plan sponsor groups, 401(k) plan industry groups, research entities, consumer groups, and six federal agencies (Consumer Financial Protection Bureau, Department of Labor, Department of the Treasury, Pension Benefit Guaranty Corporation, Securities and Exchange Commission, and Social Security Administration) about plans' use of forced-transfer IRAs and what challenges individuals and plans face related to inactive accounts and multiple accounts in the United States. We also reviewed research and industry literature, relevant laws and regulations, 2013 ERISA Advisory Council[1] testimony on missing participants, industry whitepapers on a proposed default roll-in system, and submissions to the 2013 Pension Benefit Guaranty Corporation request for information related to a tracking system for distributions from terminating plans.

To understand what happens to forced-transfer IRA accounts over time, we constructed projections of what would happen to an account balance year to year, given certain assumptions. We drew those assumptions from the actual forced-transfer IRA account terms provided by providers we interviewed and on which we collected data. We used the account opening fee, annual fee, search fees, and rate of investment return to project how long it would take for a $1,000 balance to decrease to zero. While the range of average balances transferred into forced-transfer IRAs reported by providers we interviewed was $1,850 to $3,900, we used a $1,000 balance for our projection to make it easier to observe the difference in values over time shown in the projection.[2]

Appendix III shows the projected outcome for a $1,000 balance given the fee and return information reported by the forced-transfer IRA providers we contacted.

To determine how forced-transfer IRAs are used, as described in appendix II, we projected the balance of a typical low-wage worker at the end of a typical tenure given certain assumptions about savings, investment returns, and employer matching and vesting policies. Specifically, we wanted to see if the projected balance would fall below the $5,000 cap used to determine eligibility for forced transfers. The projections assume the annual mean wage in 2013 for the service sector occupation with the most workers, specifically "food preparation and serving related occupations," including an annual raise equal to the average annual increase in wage over 15 years (1999-2013). For these assumptions, we referred to the U.S. Bureau of Labor Statistics' (BLS) Occupational Employment Statistics, National Employment and Wage Estimates. The Occupational Employment Statistics survey covers all full-time and part-time wage and salary workers in nonfarm industries. The survey does not cover the self-employed, owners and partners in unincorporated firms, household workers, or unpaid family workers. We assumed the 2014 median tenure for employed workers in the food preparation- and serving-related occupations, according to BLS data. We also assumed that employer contributions, when there were any, were made concurrently with employer contributions, rather than on a separate periodic or annual basis. These projected savings also reflect a 6.3 percent investment return, which is the geometric mean of 10-year returns for all target date funds according to our analysis of data from Morningstar.com. Target date funds are the most common default investment for individuals automatically enrolled into 401(k) plans, according to the Plan Sponsor Council of America's (55th) Annual Survey of Profit Sharing and 401(k) Plans, which reflects the 2011 plan experience. We used optimistic, moderate, and pessimistic assumptions to project vested balances (see appendix IV for additional details on our assumptions). To estimate the number and the value of accounts that could potentially be—but were not already—transferred to forced-transfer IRAs, we collected Social Security Administration (SSA) data from the form 8955-SSA. Data on the form 8955-SSA include deferred vested benefits in all defined contribution plans, including 401(k) plans, as well as in defined benefit plans, which are not subject to forced transfers. We assessed the reliability of the data and found that it met our standards, given our use of the data. We previously reported that data from the form 8955-SSA on potential private sector pension benefits retirees may be owed by former employers are not always updated or verified over time and may not reflect later distributions from plans, such as rollovers to a new plan or cash-outs. We also asked PLANSPONSOR.com to include questions about plan sponsors' use of forced transfers in its newsletter, which is distributed to online subscribers. Respondents to the query included 14 plan sponsors and 4 third-party administrators/record keepers. To assess the reliability of the data we analyzed, we reviewed IRA market data and interviewed IRA providers familiar with forced-transfer IRAs. We determined that these data were sufficiently reliable for the purposes of this report.

To better understand forced-transfer IRAs, as well as the challenges people face in keeping track of multiple 401(k) plan accounts, we also interviewed plan sponsor groups, 401(k) plan industry groups, research entities, consumer groups, and six federal agencies (Department of Labor, Department of the Treasury, Social Security Administration, Pension Benefit Guaranty Corporation (PBGC), Securities and Exchange Commission, and Consumer Financial Protection Bureau) about plans' use of forced-transfer IRAs and what challenges individuals and plans face related to multiple accounts and inactive accounts in the United States. We also reviewed research and industry literature, relevant laws and regulations, 2013 Employee Retirement Income Security Act Advisory Council testimony on missing participants, industry whitepapers on a proposed default roll-in system, and submissions to the 2013 PBGC request for information related to a tracking system for distributions from terminating plans.

To examine how other countries are addressing challenges of inactive accounts, we selected six countries to study. We considered countries with extensive workplace retirement systems to include populations that might face challenges similar to those of U.S. participants. To make our selections, we reviewed publicly available research and interviewed researchers, consumer groups, industry groups, and government agencies. We considered the extent to which countries appeared to have implemented innovative policies to help individuals keep track of their retirement savings accounts over their careers, reduce the number of forgotten or lost accounts, make such accounts easier to find, and improve outcomes for those with lost accounts. We also considered how recently legislated or implemented solutions were adopted given the increasingly powerful role information technology can play in connecting individuals with information. On the basis of this initial review, we selected six countries—Australia, Belgium, Denmark, the Netherlands, Switzerland, and the United Kingdom—that could potentially provide lessons for the United States. We interviewed government officials and industry representatives from all the selected countries. We did not conduct independent legal analyses to verify information provided about the laws or regulations in the countries selected for this study. Instead, we relied on appropriate secondary sources, interviews, and other sources to support our work. We submitted key report excerpts to agency officials in each country for their review and verification, and we incorporated their technical corrections as necessary.

We conducted this performance audit from May 2013 to November 2014 in accordance with generally accepted government auditing standards. Those standards require that we plan and perform the audit to obtain sufficient, appropriate evidence to provide a reasonable basis for our findings and conclusions based on our audit objectives. We believe that the evidence obtained provides a reasonable basis for findings and conclusions based on our audit objectives.

APPENDIX II: USE OF FORCED-TRANSFER IRAS

Active plans force out separated participants primarily to reduce plan costs, administrative burden, and liability. In response to a poll conducted by PLANSPONSOR.com through its newsletter, some respondents (made up of both plans and third party administrators) indicated that plans chose to use forced transfers for balances of $5,000 or less because they wanted to reduce costs from having additional participants who have small accounts.[1] Specifically, plans pay fees based on the total number of participants or on the average plan balance. The administrative burden on plans is another incentive to force out participants with inactive accounts, absent participant instruction, into forced-transfer IRAs. Other respondents to PLANSPONSOR.com's query reported that they used forced transfers because they wanted to reduce the complexity and administrative responsibilities associated with locating separated, non cashed-out participants. Also, small plans may wish to avoid the additional disclosure requirements and expenses associated with separated employees. In addition, active plans may opt to force out separated participants with eligible balances to reduce the plans' legal liability related to those individuals. Lastly, plans also use forced-transfer IRAs to help reduce their ongoing responsibility with regard to uncashed checks.[2]

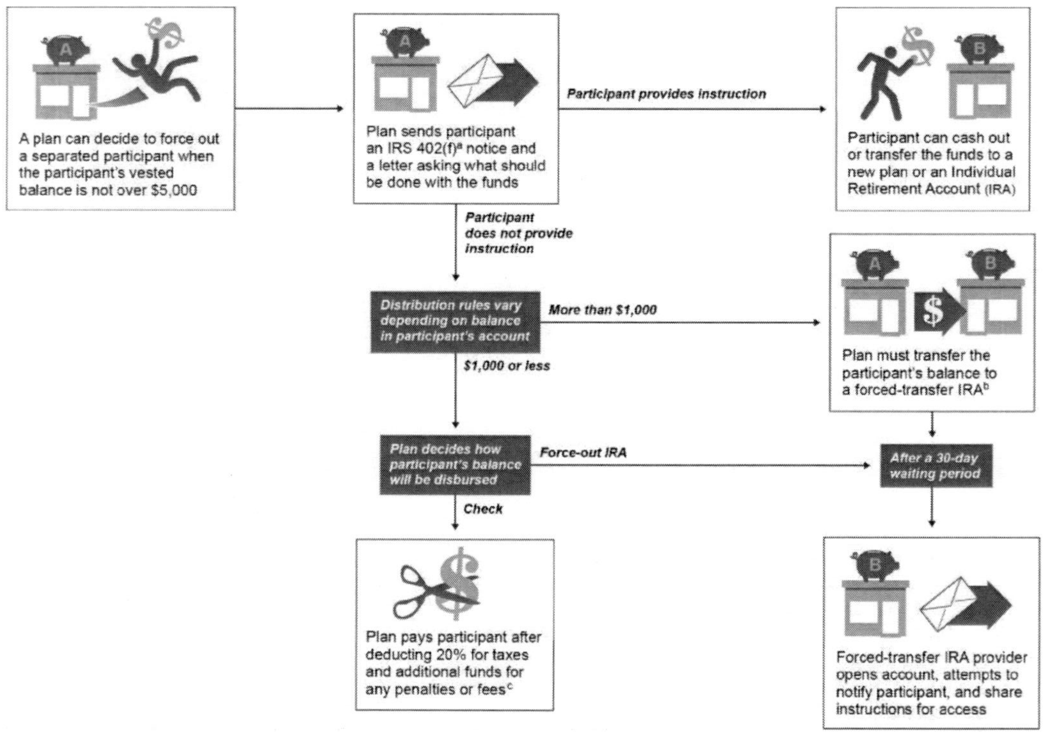

Source: GAO interviews with forced-transfer IRA providers and GAO review of select laws and regulations. | GAO-15-73.

[a] Plans are required by statute to provide participants with a written explanation of various tax consequences resulting from a distribution to the participant of funds from the plan prior to any such distribution. 26 U.S.C. § 402(f).

[b] The Economic Growth and Tax Relief Reconciliation Act of 2001 (EGTRRA) amended the law to require plans forcing out participants with balances of more than $1,000 to transfer those balances to individual retirement accounts. 26 U.S.C. § 401(a)(31)(E). The Department of Labor promulgated safe harbor regulations for such a transfer that describe the characteristics of a forced-transfer IRA. 29 C.F.R. § 2550.404a-2.

[c] The Internal Revenue Code applies a 10 percent penalty on individuals who take a taxable distribution from their plan or IRA prior to turning age of 591/2. 26 U.S.C. § 72(t).

Figure 12. Forced-Transfer IRA Process for Active 401(k) Plans.

When transferring an account into a forced-transfer IRA, a plan must first notify the participant of its intention to forcibly transfer the account and that if the participant does not instruct otherwise, the account will be transferred into a forced-transfer IRA.[3] An example of such a notice is shown in appendix V. See figure 12 for an example of how the forced-transfer IRA process works for active 401(k) plans.

Although a plan must try to locate a missing participant before seeking to force the participant out of the plan, actually forcing such a participant out of the plan and initiating the forced transfer to an IRA does not require any additional last-ditch efforts to locate the participant.[4] For example, a plan might get back some returned plan communications mailed to a separated participant and search unsuccessfully for an updated address. Later, when that plan sweeps out the balances of separated participants, the plan is not required to search again for the missing participant. Instead, efforts to locate the missing participant are at the discretion of the provider and generally at the expense of the individual participant's balance.[5]

Active 401(k) Plans Forcibly Transfer Billions of Dollars in Separated Participants' Savings

One industry survey shows that about half of active 401(k) plans force out separated participants with balances of $1,000 to $5,000.[6] We collected forced-transfer IRA account data from 10 IRA providers that have, together, opened more than 1.8 million forced-transfer IRA accounts totaling $3.4 billion in retirement savings, as of 2013.[7] One of the largest forced-transfer IRA providers has projected that more than 600,000 new forced-transfer IRAs could be created each year, given attrition rates, the percentage of vested balances under $5,000, and the rate of non-responsiveness among separating participants faced with making a distribution choice. Based on that estimate and assuming an average account balance of $2,500 (half of the $5,000 cap), a total of $1.5 billion would be transferred into these accounts each year.

Data provided by SSA are consistent with those estimates. From 2004 to 2013, separated participants left more than 16 million accounts of $5,000 or less in workplace retirement plans, with an aggregate value of $8.5 billion.[8] Those data reflect both defined contribution and defined benefit plans, but even if a portion of the accounts are in defined contribution plans, it suggests that there are millions of accounts and billions in savings that could be transferred to IRAs if those plans choose to retroactively force transfer eligible accounts.[9]

Although the plans reflected in SSA's data had not yet forcibly transferred these small accounts, the defined contribution plans may still do so. For example, a plan may choose to sweep out eligible accounts once a year or on some periodic basis.

Plans' use of forced-transfer IRAs is also increasing. Some forced-transfer IRA providers have seen the number of new forced-transfer IRAs increase each year. In addition, the largest of the specialty providers we interviewed said that the number of new forced-transfer IRAs that they administered increased nearly 300 percent over 5 years, from 26,011 new accounts in 2008 to 103,229 in 2012.[10] They expect that upward trend to continue. Industry professionals also said that the wider use of automatic enrollment has the potential to result in greater use of forced-transfer IRAs, as participants who are relatively unengaged, and thus less likely to make a choice about where to transfer their savings, are forced out by plans when they separate.

Finally, some plans do not yet force out participants because their plan documents do not, as required, [11] include provisions for forcing them out and transferring their eligible 401(k) plan accounts into forced-transfer IRAs. The PSCA survey of 401(k) plans stated that about 40 percent of plans do not currently force out participants with balances of $1,000 to $5,000.[12] If these plans begin to use forced transfers, they can force out participants with eligible balances going forward and go back and sweep out participants who left small accounts years ago. Thus, anyone with a small balance left with a past employer's 401(k) plan could find themselves notified of the plan's intention to force them out—no matter how long ago their separation—and of a potential transfer to an forced-transfer IRA.

Forced-Transfer IRAs Are Used to a Lesser Extent by Terminating Plans

Several forced-transfer IRA providers we spoke with said that forced transfers from terminating plans represent a small part of their forced-transfer IRA business. For example, one provider said that terminated plan transfers constitute 9 percent of the provider's forced-transfer IRAs. Some providers do not offer forced-transfer IRAs to terminating plans. One of the largest providers told us that it offers forced-transfer IRAs as an accommodation to ongoing plan sponsor clients, but typically does not offer them if the plan is terminating. [13] In some cases, forced-transfer IRA providers will provide the accounts for terminating plans that cannot secure a contract with a larger service provider.

Despite the limited use of forced-transfer IRAs by terminating plans, they have prescriptive requirements[14] for notifying participants prior to the forced transfer of balances, which include using certified mail, reviewing other employee benefit plan records for more up-to-date information, and contacting the designated beneficiary to get more accurate contact information. As a result, participants in terminating plans are more likely to have an opportunity to select a distribution destination other than a forced-transfer IRA or individual retirement annuity.

APPENDIX III: PROJECTED OUTCOME OF A $1,000 BALANCE LEFT IN A FORCED-TRANSFER IRA FOR 30 YEARS

Through interviews, data requests, and web research we collected forced-transfer IRA terms for 10 forced-transfer IRA providers. Almost all providers offer varying account terms for different forced-transfer IRAs. In all, there were 19 different account terms from the 10 providers for which we collected data. We collected data on account opening fees, initial address search fees, ongoing account fees, ongoing address search fees, and investment returns. Some forced-transfer IRA providers also charge fees for certain transactions, including distributions and account closings, but we did not incorporate them into our projections, which show the effect of the account terms if the account holder takes no action and the balance remains in the forced-transfer IRA. While not all forced-transfer IRA terms result in the balance decreasing to $0 over 30 years, the growth of those account balances is less than would have resulted had the funds been invested in a typical target date fund. In contrast to the projected outcomes shown in table 7, the projected balance of $1,000 in a forced-transfer IRA with a $6.75 set-up fee, a $42 annual fee (the median fees among the combinations we reviewed), and a 6.30 percent average target date return,[1] would be $2,708 after 30 years or growth of 173 percent.

Table 7. The Projected Balance of a $1,000 Forced-Transfer IRA after 30 years, Given 19 Combinations of Account Fees and Investment Returns for 10 Providers

Time to decrease to $0	... or, the balance remaining after 30 years	Terms of the Forced-Transfer IRA, including fees	Investment returns
9 years	$0	$50 set up fee; $50 annual fee; $65 annual search fee, 0.01 % of assets	0.11%
9 years	$0	$50 set up fee; $50 annual fee; $65 annual search fee; 0.01 % of assets	0.04%
9 years	$0	$50 set up fee; $50 annual fee; $65 annual search fee, 0.01 % of assets	1.5%
9 years	$0	$50 set up fee; $50 annual fee; $65 annual search fee, 0.01 % of assets	0.15%
15 years	$0	No set up fee; $60 annual fee; $18 annual search fee; 0.35% assets fee	2.05%
20 years	$0	20% balance set up fee, $45 annual fee	1.0%
22 years	$0	$30 set up fee; $45 annual fee	0.05%
24 years	$0	No set up fee; $3.50 per month ($42 per year) account fee	0.05%
24 years	$0	No set up fee; $45 annual fee	0.01%
25 years	$0	No set up fee, $35 initial search fee, $45 annual fee	1.0%
29 years	$0	$10 set up fee, $35 annual fee	0.05%
29 years	$0	No set up fee, $35 annual fee	0.01%
29 years	$0	No set up fee, $35 annual fee	0.05%
	$422	No set up fee, $20 annual fee	0.1%
	$553	$25 set up fee, $15 annual fee	0.12%
	$572	$25 set up fee, $15 annual fee	0.2%
	($996.50) a	No set up fee, $3.50 initial search fee, $35 annual fee or capped at return	0.5%
	$1,006	No set up fee; no annual fee	0.02%
	$1,678	No set up fee; no annual fee	1.74%

Source: GAO analysis of forced-transfer IRA account fee and return data collected for ten providers. | GAO-15-73.

Notes: Percentage is shown by the sign '%'. The gray line distinguishes those 17 combinations of fees and investment returns that resulted in a decreased value over time versus those 2 that resulted in some increase in value over time. Actual annual returns would not remain the same for 30 years, they could go up or down, but these projections reflect what could happen given the most recent returns reported by providers.

[a] In this scenario the balance neither increases nor decreases over time because—unless the return exceeds the $35 annual fee—the fee is capped at the return, which is just $4.98 each year on a $996.50 balance.

APPENDIX IV: PROJECTED VESTED RETIREMENT SAVINGS OF A LOW-WAGE 401(K) PLAN PARTICIPANT GIVEN PESSIMISTIC, MODERATE, AND OPTIMISTIC ASSUMPTIONS (TABLE)

Vested balance after 2.2 year tenure assuming a policy of…				
	Immediate vesting	3-year cliff vestingd	5-year graduated vestingd	6-year graduated vestingd
Pessimistica 3% employee contribution, no employer match (so vesting is not relevant), 6-month service requirement	$1,282	$1,282	$1,282	$1,282
Moderateb 3% employee contribution, 50% employer match up to 6% of salary, 3-month service requirement	$2,214	$1,476	$1,661	$1,624
Optimisticc 5.2% employee contribution, 50% employer match up to 6% of salary, no service requirement	$4,344	$2,896	$3,258	$3,185

Source: GAO projections based on analysis of industry and government data. | GAO-15-73.

Notes: The projections assume the annual mean wage in 2013 ($21,580) for the service sector occupation with the most workers, specifically “food preparation and serving related occupations,” including an annual raise of 2.36 percent, which is the average annual increase in wage over 15 years (1999-2013). For these assumptions, we referred to the U.S. Bureau of Labor Statistics’ (BLS) Occupational Employment Statistics, National Employment and Wage Estimates. We assumed a 2.2 year tenure, which is the 2014 median tenure for employed workers in the food preparation- and serving-related occupations, according to BLS data. We also assumed that employer contributions, when there were any, were made concurrently with employer contributions, rather than on a separate periodic or annual basis. More than half of defined contribution plans (such as 401(k) plans) are in the service sector and about 40 percent of defined contribution plan participants work in the service sector, according to 2011 data published by the Employee Benefits Security Administration. These projected savings also reflect a 6.3 percent investment return, which is the geometric mean of 10 year returns for all target date funds according to our analysis of data from Morningstar.com. Target date funds are the most popular default investment for individuals automatically enrolled into 401(k) plans, according to the PSCA's *55th Annual Survey of Profit Sharing and 401(k) Plans*, which reflects the 2011 plan experience.

[a] Pessimistic assumptions: This projection assumes a 3 percent employee contribution, no employer match, and a 6-month service requirement. About 54 percent of plans that automatically enroll employees in a retirement savings plan set a default deferral of 3 percent of salary and 30 percent of plans offer no matching employer contribution, according to the PSCA's *55th Annual Survey of Profit Sharing and 401(k) Plans*.

According to the same source, about 20 percent of plans have a service requirement of 6 months or more. The pessimistic projections do not vary depending on the vesting schedule because there is no employer contribution assumed in this scenario and only employer contributions, and investment returns thereon, are affected by vesting rules. Employee contributions are always immediately vested.

[b] Moderate assumptions: This projection assumes a 3 percent employee contribution, a 50 percent employer match, and a 3-month service requirement. About 54 percent of plans that automatically enroll employees in a plan set a default deferral of 3 percent of salary and 48 percent of plans offer a 50 percent match, according to data from the PSCA's *55th Annual Survey of Profit Sharing and 401(k) Plans*. According to the same source, 16.6 percent of plans reported a service requirement of 3 months.

[c] Optimistic assumptions: We assumed a 5.2 percent employee contribution, a 50 percent match, and no service requirement. The average pre-tax salary deferral among non-highly compensated workers in 2011 was 5.2 percent. A 50 percent match is used by 48 percent of plans, according to data from the PSCA's *55th Annual Survey of Profit Sharing and 401(k) Plans*. The same source shows that 60 percent of plans have no service requirement.

d Vesting schedules:

- Under 3-year cliff vesting, the employer's contribution and investment returns thereon are 100 percent vested after 3 years of service.
- Under graduated vesting, the employer's contribution and investment returns thereon are partially vested after each year of service, depending on how long the graduated vesting period is. In our projections, we used:

- for a 5-year vesting schedule: 0, 25, 50, 75, 100 percent and the ends of years 2 through 5; and
- for a 6-year gradated vesting schedule:0, 20, 40, 60, 80, and 100 percent at the end of years 2 through 6.

APPENDIX V: EXAMPLE NOTIFICATION OF PLAN FORCED-TRANSFER POLICY

[redacted]

ENV#MIN000001
CUSTOMER SAMPLE
400 PURITAN WAY
CAMPBELLSBURG KY 40011

Action Deadline: 05/25/2012
Cash Distribution Limit: $ 5,000.00

04/05/2012

RE: NAME OF CLIENT
99999

Dear CUSTOMER SAMPLE:

IMPORTANT NOTICE: ACTION MAY BE REQUIRED BY 4PM EASTERN TIME 05/25/2012
We are writing in respect to your retirement account in the Plan listed above. As part of a periodic review, **your account has been identified as having a vested market value equal to or less than your Plan's minimum required balance** of $5000.

Vested Account Balance (subject to distribution): $.77

In accordance with Plan provisions your vested account balance will be distributed from the Plan. No action is required unless you would like to elect a different distribution option than what is outlined below. If you do not elect to receive a distribution prior to the action deadline listed above, your account will be distributed as follows:

If you have attained the later of age 62 or your Plan's normal retirement age, your account will be liquidated and a cash distribution will be made to you in the form of a check. As required by federal tax law, 20% of the taxable portion of your distribution will be withheld (state tax withholding may also apply).
If you have not yet attained the later of age 62 or your Plan's normal retirement age, your account will be distributed as follows:
If your balance is less than or equal to $1,000, a cash distribution will be made to you in the form of a check. As required by federal tax law, 20% of the taxable portion of your distribution will be withheld (state tax withholding may also apply).
If your balance is greater than $1,000, the Plan provides that your vested account balance be rolled over to an Individual Retirement Account (IRA) at . Your rollover will be placed in the fund until you provide other direction. Important additional information for participants with Roth and non-Roth balances (Roth may not be offered by your plan):
The $1,000 rollover limit is applied separately to the Roth and non-Roth balances. If either your Roth balance or your non-Roth balance is equal to or less than $1,000, you will receive a check for that balance.
Example 1) if your account has a $2,000 balance comprised of $1,500 of non-Roth money and $500 of Roth money, you will receive a check for the $500 of Roth money, and the $1,500 of non-Roth money will be rolled over to an IRA.
Example 2) if your account has a $900 balance comprised of $400 of non-Roth money and $500 of Roth money, then you would receive two checks as each falls under the $1,000 limit to be automatically rolled over.
Example 3) if your account has a $1,500 Roth balance and a $1,500 non-Roth balance, $1,500 will be rolled over to a traditional IRA and $1,500 will be rolled over to a Roth IRA.

Because the value of your account can fluctuate, changes in value prior to payment may change how your account is handled. The account balance on the "automatic distribution date" will determine if your account is to be cashed out or (if it exceeds the Plan's minimum) remain in the Plan - not the value of the vested account balance when this letter was issued.

If you will be age 70 1/2 on or before December 31st, a portion of your distribution is required to be taken as cash and is not eligible to be rolled into another retirement account. This amount satisfies the Minimum Required Distribution (MRD) mandated by the IRS. If you elect to rollover a portion of your funds, a service representative will inform you of your MRD amount that is not rollover eligible.

Enclosed you will find a Special Tax Notice regarding plan payments for your reference. You may contact [redacted] to request a distribution prior to the action deadline noted above. You may log onto your account at netbenefits.com to review and select distribution options. For additional service you may call 1-800-[redacted] between service hours Weekdays 8:30 a.m. - Midnight ET. Please be sure to understand the tax consequences of any distributions from the Plan. In the event of a discrepancy between the process outlined in this letter and the terms of the Plan document, the Plan document shall control.

Company, Inc.

0000099999000002

Page 1 of 1

APPENDIX VI: SELECTED REPORTING AND DISCLOSURE REQUIREMENTS AT PARTICIPANT SEPARATION AND CERTAIN PLAN EVENTS (TABLE)

	Sending entity	Receiving entity	Form	Summary description of form contents
Cash-out at separation	Plan	Internal Revenue Service (IRS) and Participant	1099-R, Distributions From Pensions, Annuities, Retirement or Profit-Sharing Plans, IRAs, Insurance Contracts, etc, 26 U.S.C. § 6047(d). 26 C.F.R. § 31.3405(c)-1.	Reports distributions made from retirement plans and Individual Retirement Accounts (IRA). (*Note: The form specifies if the distribution was a direct rollover,b including those from forced transfers, butit does not specify if the distribution went to a plan or IRA, or to a forced-transfer IRA.)* Due to participant by January 31st following the calendar year of the distribution and to IRS by February 28th of the year following the calendar year of the distribution.
	Plan	Participant	402(f) Special Tax Notice (or Rollover Notice), 26 U.S.C. § 402(f)(1)	Explains the tax implications of the different distribution options, including explanation of the rollover rules, the special tax treatment for cash-outs (also called lump-sum distributions), and the mandatory withholding of 20 percent of distributions (including those that result in an indirect rollover).[c]
	Plan	Participant *Only required for balances over $5,000.	Notice of Right to Defer Distribution (Or Participant Consent Notice), 26 C.F.R. § 1.411(a)-11(c) .	Notifies participant of right to defer receipt of an immediately distributable benefit. To obtain participant's consent to distribution in excess of $5,000 prior to plan's normal retirement age (NRA), participant must be given a description of the plan's distribution options and be informed of right to defer distribution and the consequences offailing to defer.[d]

Appendix VI. (Continued)

	Sending entity	Receiving entity	Form	Summary description of form contents
Remains in plan at separation	Plan	IRS	8955-SSA, Annual Registration Statement Identifying Separated Participants with Deferred Vested Benefits, 26 U.S.C. § 6057(a).	Reports separated participants with deferred vested benefits remaining in the plan and includesname of plan and plan contact information as well as the value of the account. (Note: The plan sends the 8955-SSA to IRS, IRS then sends it to SSA.)
	Plan	Participant	Individual Statement of Deferred Vested Retirement Benefit	Includes same information as the 8955-SSA; plan name, name and address of plan administrator, name of participant, nature, amount and form of the deferred vested benefit.
Transferred to forced-transfer IRA at separation	Plan	IRS and Participant	1099-R, Distributions From Pensions, Annuities, Retirement or Profit-Sharing Plans, IRAs, Insurance Contracts, etc, 26 U.S.C. § 6047(d). 26 C.F.R. § 31.3405(c)-1.	Reports distributions made from retirement plans and IRAs. (Note: The form specifies if the distribution was a direct rollover,bincluding those from forced transfers, but it does not specify if the distribution went to a plan or IRA, or to a forced-transfer IRA.) Due to participant by January 31st following the calendar year of the distribution and to IRS by February 28th of the year following the calendar year of the distribution.

	Sending entity	Receiving entity	Form	Summary description of form contents
	Plan	Participant	402(f) Special Tax Notice (or Rollover Notice), 26 U.S.C. § 402(f)(1)	Explains the tax implications of the different distribution options, including explanation of the rollover rules, the special tax treatment for cashouts (also called lump-sum distributions), and the mandatory withholding of 20 percent of distributions (including those that result in an indirect rollover).[c]
	Plan	Participant	Automatic Rollover Notice	Notifies participant that, absent any participant instructions, a distribution will be paid to an individual retirement plan.[e]
	IRA	IRS and Participant	5498, IRA Contribution Information	Reports contributions, rollovers, transfers, and recharacterizations, as well as the fair market value and whether a required minimum distribution is required.
Rollover to new plan	Plan	IRS and Participant	1099-R, Distributions From Pensions, Annuities, Retirement or Profit-Sharing Plans, IRAs, Insurance Contracts, etc, 26 U.S.C. § 6047(d). 26 C.F.R. § 31.3405(c)-1.	Reports distributions made from retirement plans and IRAs. (Note: The form specifies if the distribution was a direct rollover,[b] including those from forced transfers, but it does not specify if the distribution went to a plan or IRA, or to a forcedtransfer IRA.) Due to participant by January 31st following the calendar year of the distribution and to IRS by February 28th of the year following the calendar year of the distribution.

Appendix VI. (Continued)

	Sending entity	Receiving entity	Form	Summary description of form contents
	Plan	Participant	402(f) Special Tax Notice (or Rollover Notice), 26 U.S.C. § 402(f)(1)	Explains the tax implications of the different distribution options, including explanation of the rollover rules, the special tax treatment for cashouts (also called lump-sum distributions), and the mandatory withholding of 20 percent of distributions (including those that result in an indirect rollover).[c]
	Plan	Participant *Only required for balances over $5,000.	Notice of Right to Defer Distribution (Or Participant Consent Notice), 26 C.F.R. § 1.411(a)-11(c) (2012).	Notifies participant of right to defer receipt of an immediately distributable benefit. To obtain participant's consent to distribution in excess of $5,000 prior to plan's NRA, participant must be given a description of the plan's distribution options and be informed of right to defer distribution and the consequences of failing to defer.[d]
Rollover to IRA	Plan	IRS and Participant	1099-R, Distributions From Pensions, Annuities, Retirement or Profit-Sharing Plans, IRAs, Insurance Contracts, etc, 26 U.S.C. § 6047(d). 26 C.F.R. § 31.3405(c)-1.	Reports distributions made from retirement plans and IRAs. (Note: The form specifies if the distribution was a direct rollover,[b] including those from forced transfers, but it does not specify if the distribution went to a plan or IRA, or to a forcedt ransfer IRA.) Due to participant by January 31st following the calendar year of the distribution and to IRS by February 28th of the year following the calendar year of the distribution.
	Plan	Participant	402(f) Special Tax Notice (or Rollover Notice), 26 U.S.C. § 402(f)(1)	Explains the tax implications of the different distribution options, including explanation of the rollover rules, the special tax treatment for cash-outs (also called lump-sum distributions), and the mandatory withholding of 20 percent of distributions (including those that result in an indirect rollover).[c]

	Sending entity	Receiving entity	Form	Summary description of form contents
	Plan	Participant *Only required for balances over $5,000.	Notice of Right to Defer Distribution (*Or Participant Consent Notice)*, 26 C.F.R. § 1.411(a)-11(c) (2012).	Notifies participant of right to defer receipt of an immediately distributable benefit. To obtain participant's consent to distribution in excess of $5,000 prior to plan's NRA, participant must be given a description of the plan's distribution options and be informed of right to defer distribution and the consequences of failing to defer.[d]
	IRA	IRS and Participant	Form 5498, IRA Contribution Information	Reports contributions, rollovers, transfers, and recharacterizations, as well as the fair market value and whether a required minimum distribution is required.
Plan termination	Plan	IRS	5310, Application for Determination for Terminating Plans	Optional request for a determination on the plan's qualification status at the time of the plan's termination.
	Plan	Participant	Notice to Interested Parties Rev. Proc. 2013-6, 2013-1 I.R.B. 198, corrected by Ann. 2013-13, 2013-9 I.R.B. 532	Notifies employees, participants and beneficiaries that an application for determination is being submitted to the IRS and of their right to comment on the plan. Notice must be posted or sent (electronic media permissible) before the application is submitted to the IRS—between 10 and 24 days of the application date.

Appendix VI. (Continued)

	Sending entity	Receiving entity	Form	Summary description of form contents
	Plan	Participant	Notice of Plan Termination	Notifies participants and beneficiaries of the plan'stermination and distribution options and procedures to make an election. In addition, the notice must provide information about the account balance; explain, if known, what fees, if any, will be paid from the participant or beneficiary's retirement plan; and provide the name, address and telephone number of the individual retirement plan provider, if known, and of the plan administrator or other fiduciary from whom information about the termination may be obtained. See 29 C.F.R. § 2550.404a-3. The notice will be given during the winding up process of the plan termination. Participants and beneficiaries have 30 days from the receipt of the notice to elect a form of distribution.
	Plan	Department of Labor (DOL), IRS, Pension Benefit Guaranty Corporation (PBGC)	Final Form 5500, Annual Return/Report of Employee Benefit Plan (including any applicable schedules) 26 U.S.C. § 6058(a). 29 U.S.C. § 1024.	Indicates when all assets under the plan have been distributed when "final return/report" box on the form 5500 is checked. Indicates that all assetswere distributed and current value of assets at thedate of distribution via schedule H (for plans with 100 or more participants) and schedule I (plans with less than 100 participants).

	Sending entity	Receiving entity	Form	Summary description of form contents
Plan merger, etc.	Plan	IRS	5310-A, Notice of Plan Merger or Consolidation, Spinoff, or Transfer of Plan Assets or Liabilities; Notice of Qualified Separate Lines of Business	Gives notice of certain plan mergers, consolidations, spinoffs or transfers of assets or liabilities from one plan to another. Each plan with a separate EIN and plan number involved in merger or transfer of assets or liabilities must file. For spinoffs, only plan in existence before spinoff must file.[f] Form must be filed at least 30 days prior to a merger, consolidation, spinoff, or transfers of plan assets or liabilities to another plan.
	Plan (a plan that is terminated as a result of a merger)	DOL, IRS, and PBGC	Final Form 5500, Annual Return/Report of Employee Benefit Plan (including any applicable schedules) 26 U.S.C. § 6058(a). 29 U.S.C. § 1024.	Indicates when all assets under the plan have been distributed when "final return/report" box on the form 5500 is checked. Indicates that all assetswere distributed and current value of assets at thedate of distribution via schedule H (for plans with 100 or more participants) and schedule I (plans with less than 100 participants), Schedules H and I also provide the net value of all assets transferred to and from the plan, including those resulting from mergers and spinoffs.
	Plan (New Plan)	Participant	Notification	Includes the new plan sponsor's name and address.

Source: GAO analysis of laws and regulations. | GAO-15-73.

[a] We use the term "cash out" to refer to a lump-sum distribution made to an employee at job separation that is not subsequently rolled over into a qualified employer plan or IRA.

[b] The Internal Revenue Code (IRC) requires that participants with an eligible rollover distribution have the option to roll their distributions into an IRA or another employer's tax-qualified plan in the form of a direct rollover. 26 U.S.C. § 401(a)(31)(A).

[c] IRS regulations generally require plans to provide the notice no less than 30 and no more than 90 days before the date of distribution. 26 C.F.R. § 1.402(f)-1, Q/A-2, Q/A-5) (2012). The Pension Protection Act of 2006 (PPA) directed the regulations be changed to "no more than 180 days" (Pub. L. No. 109-280, § 1102(a)(1)(B), 120 Stat. 780, 1056) but the rule IRS proposed (73 Fed. Reg. 59,575 (Oct. 9, 2008)), per PPA, has not been finalized.

[d] IRS regulations generally require plans to also provide this information to participants no less than 30 and no more than 90 days before the date of distribution. PPA directed the regulations be changed to "no more than 180 days" (Pub. L. No. 109-280, § 1102(a)(1)(B), 120 Stat. 780, 1056.), but the rule IRS proposed (73 Fed. Reg. 59,575 (Oct. 9, 2008)), per PPA, has not been finalized. The same proposed rule modifies the regulations under section 411(a)(11) of the IRC to provide that the description of a participant's right, if any, to defer receipt of a distribution shall also describe the consequences of failing to defer such receipt. (73 Fed. Reg. 59,576) Additionally, under the proposed regulation plans would be required to include in the information provided, among other things, statements that: "some currently available investment options in the plan may not be generally available on similar terms outside the plan and contact information for obtaining additional information on the general availability outside the plan of currently available investment options in the plan," and "fees and expenses (including administrative or investment-related fees) outside the plan may be different from fees and expenses that apply to the participant's account and contact information for obtaining information on such fees." 73 Fed. Reg.

[e] The Economic Growth and Tax Relief Reconciliation Act of 2001 added the notice provision and required the plan administrator notify the distributee in writing (either separately or as part of the § 402(f) notice). Pub. L. No. 107-16, § 657, 115 Stat.38, 135 (codified at 26 U.S.C. §§ 401(a)(31)(B) and 402(f)(1)(A)). In addition, to meet the conditions of DOL's safe harbor and therefore, be deemed to have satisfied their fiduciary duties with regard to mandatory distributions, plans must provide participants with a summary plan description, or a summary of material modifications, meeting certain requirements. Specifically, it must describe the plan's forced-transfer IRA provisions (including an explanation that the forced-transfer IRA will be invested in an investment product designed to preserve principal and provide a reasonable rate of return and liquidity), a description of how fees and expense attendant to the individual retirement plan will be allocated (i.e., the extent to which expenses will be borne by the account holder alone or shared with the distributing plan or plan sponsor), and the name, address and phone number of a plan contact (to the extent not otherwise provided). 29 C.F.R. § 2550.404a-2.

[f] Exceptions: Form should not be filed for eligible rollover distributions paid directly to an eligible retirement plan, or for mergers, consolidations, or spinoffs meeting certain requirements (See IRS instructions for Form 5310-A).

APPENDIX VII: RELEVANT FEATURES OF PENSION SYSTEMS IN THE SIX COUNTRIES SELECTED FOR THIS REPORT

This appendix provides additional details on the six countries we studied and their approach to managing challenges posed by inactive retirement accounts. In making our selection we considered countries with extensive workplace retirement systems to include populations that might face challenges similar to those of U.S. participants, and considered the extent to which such countries had recent or innovative approaches to address the challenges posed by inactive retirement accounts. We determined that six countries could potentially provide lessons for the United States. Information on each of the following countries is included in this appendix.

- Australia
- Belgium
- Denmark
- The Netherlands
- Switzerland
- The United Kingdom

Australia

At a Glance

Since 2005, individuals in Australia have been able to select a plan (super) of their choosing to which employers they have throughout their career will contribute. However, workers not actively choosing a plan may accumulate accounts in multiple plans selected by their employers. According to Australian Treasury officials, many Australians lose track of their accounts, especially when they change jobs, names, and addresses. Small balances may be eaten away by fees, necessitating forced-transfers to preserve their value.

Forced Transfers

Since 2012, all small lost accounts under AUD 2,000 are transferred to the ATO where they become part of consolidated revenues but are credited a return equal to inflation to preserve value, when claimed. ATO officials said they plan to increase the small lost account threshold to AUD 4,000 in 2015 and AUD 6,000 in 2016. ATO officials noted that this policy is in place because the ATO has the capability to find people and match them with lost accounts through updated tax data and can prevent lost accounts from being reduced by fees. Lost accounts are transferred to the ATO when they meet certain criteria, but the most common reasons, in addition to a balance below AUD 2,000, is when the missing participant turns 65, according to Australian government officials.

Pension Registry

The Australian Tax Office (ATO) has established an online tool called SuperSeeker that individuals can use to find lost retirement accounts, via the governmental portal myGov. A smart phone application is also available for accessing the information.

Information provided to participants can be used for retirement planning purposes, including consolidation, in order to improve participant retirement security. However, The SuperSeeker does not perform analytical tasks, such as showing retirement outcomes under various scenarios, according to government officials we interviewed. Participants who find lost accounts upon searching for them are able to consolidate them online in a plan of their choice generally within 3 working days. The SuperSeeker now allows paperless "point and click" consolidation. According to ATO, nearly 155,000 accounts were consolidated in 2013-14 with a total value of about AUD 765 million. In addition, the number of lost accounts went down by 30 percent between June 2013 and June 2014.

The pension registry is primarily financed through a tax on the superannuation sector, and in some cases such as funding the letter campaign to raise awareness, from general revenue. The tax has fluctuated between AUD 2.4 million in 2002 and AUD 7.3 million in 2011, according to the ATO.

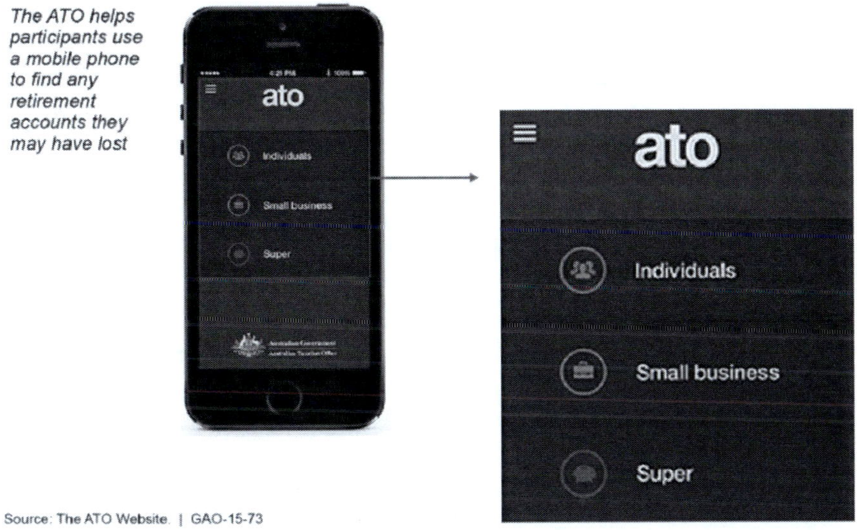

Figure 13. Screenshot of the Australian Tax Office (ATO) Mobile Phone Application.

Belgium

At a Glance

Officials told us participants changing jobs can leave their pension account behind or roll it over (1) to the plan of the new employer, (2) to a "welcome-structure" for outgoing workers often taking the form of a group insurance, or (3) to a qualified individual insurance contract. Sectoral industry plans, negotiated in collective bargaining agreements, allow participants who change jobs but stay in the same industry to keep one retirement account, according to officials. With defined benefit plans, vested benefits in dormant accounts are frozen (i.e. not subject to further cost of living or wage increases) officials told us, whereas with defined contribution plans, separated participants' dormant accounts receive the same return as active accounts but the minimum return obligation that the plan sponsor must meet, currently set at 3.25 percent of account balances per year, is frozen.

Forced Transfers

There are no forced-transfers in Belgium, officials said. When an individual separates from a plan, his or her account is kept dormant in the plan by default, according to Belgian officials; plans are required to accept transfers of inactive accounts if a participant requests it but these are kept separately from the active account.

Pension Registry

The pension registry in Belgium has two components, according to officials: a database of national pensions (similar to Social Security) and one covering workplace retirement accounts, which includes both active and inactive accounts. The pension registry does not have information on personal retirement savings. Since the enactment of legislation in 2006, the Belgian government has been collecting data on workplace accounts for private sector participants and the self-employed, according to officials. The pension registry extracts some information from existing databases (such as the registry of individuals and employers), and data from service providers, officials said. The registry stores some of the information in its database.

From 2016, the new pension registry will take over the provision of information on inactive accounts, as indicated in the law adopted in May 2014, according to Belgian officials, and workers with inactive accounts will no longer receive statements from plan sponsors or pension institutions but will be able to consult the registry online. Officials also told us the registry will help the government gather up-to-date information on retirement plans. The government finances the pension registry from general revenue, officials said.

Once fully functional, the annual cost of running the registry will be around 3.5 million euro, according to Belgian pension registry officials we interviewed.

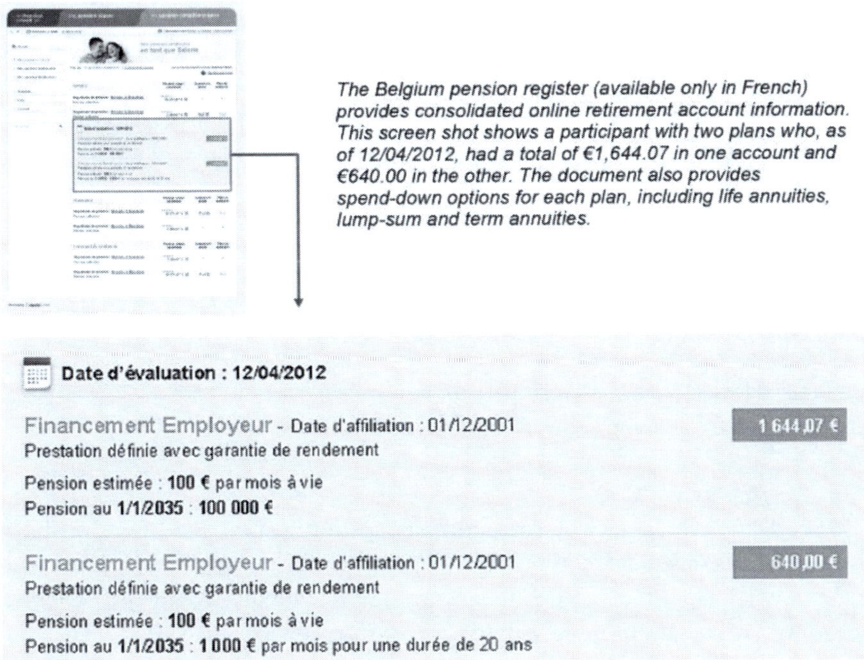

Source: Gigedis. | GAO-15-73.

Figure 14. Screenshot from Belgium Pension Registry.

Denmark

At a Glance

Multi-employer industry plans (one plan covers all workers in an industry) allow participants who change jobs but stay in the same industry to use just one retirement account. When individuals change industries, the account remains inactive in the plan, unless the participant takes action to roll it in to the new industry plan, according to Danish officials. Plans sign agreements requiring them to accept transfers requested by participants.

Danish officials said small inactive accounts are sometimes reduced and eliminated by fees. If participants never take action to consolidate accounts, plans will eventually use a participant's designated "easy access" bank account to make distribution payments at the participant's retirement age, according to Danish officials.

Forced Transfers

There is not yet a forced-transfer mechanism that consolidates inactive accounts. However, the government is considering one for small accounts to prevent them from being reduced by fees, according to Danish officials.

Pension Registry

The Danish Insurance Association's pension registry called PensionsInfo collects and consolidates retirement savings information from plans and insurers when a participant logs-in, according to materials provided by Danish Insurance Association representatives we interviewed. It stores only the government-issued identification numbers of participants in each plan.

PensionsInfo, the Danish pension register, provides current online retirement account information. The left column ("Din pension" means "your pension") shows retirement amounts starting at age 60 and continuing through age 67. The column on the right shows the corresponding lump sum payment (or "Engangsudbetaling") the user is entitled to for each retirement age. In this example, the participant retiring at age 60 would be entitled to a lump sum of 52.000 kr., or about $9,000.

Din pension	Engangsudbetaling
60 år - du går på pension som 60-årig	52.000 kr.
61 år - du går på pension som 61-årig	53.300 kr.
62 år - du går på pension som 62-årig	54.700 kr.
63 år - du går på pension som 63-årig	56.000 kr.
64 år - du går på pension som 64-årig	57.400 kr.
65 år - du går på pension som 65-årig	58.900 kr.
66 år - du går på pension som 66-årig	60.400 kr.
67 år - du går på pension som 67-årig	61.900 kr.

Source: Pensionsinfo website (www.pensionsinfo.dk). | GAO-15-73.

Figure 15. PensionsInfo Screenshot Showing Lump Sums Available at Various Retirement Ages.

Individuals can view contact information for each plan or insurer, which they can use to consolidate accounts. It is voluntary for providers to allow access to their records, but virtually all do, including government authorities who provide information on national (Social-Security-like) retirement benefits. PensionsInfo provides current account balances and projected future distribution amounts for public, workplace and private retirement benefits under various scenarios, for example, comparing lump-sum withdrawals, phased withdrawals and whole life annuities at different retirement ages. Inactive accounts can be flagged for participants in a pop-up window recommending consolidation, according to officials at the Danish Insurance Association. Participants can print or save the consolidated account information for their records, share it with a personal financial advisor, or use it in conjunction with retirement planning software designed to work with it. Insurers and plans voluntarily pay for the pension registry. The fee paid by each is calculated on the basis of the number of participants requesting to view data from them.

Recent data from the European Actuarial Consultative Group indicate that the number of unique visitors to the registry has increased from 512,218 in 2010 to 742,426 in 2011 to reach 1,132,488 in 2012. The annual cost of maintaining the pension registry is estimated at 1.5 million euro.

The Netherlands

At a Glance

Multi-employer industry plans, in which a single plan generally covers employees in one industry, allow participants who change jobs but stay in the same industry to keep one pension account. According to an Organization for

Economic Co-operation and Development Working Paper, about three quarters of workers belong to industry wide multi-employer plans.

Participants changing jobs can leave their retirement account behind or roll it over to the plan of the new employer, according to Dutch officials, although in recent years, the transfer of many defined benefit pensions has been frozen due to underfunding in those plans.

Participants receive an annual Uniform Pension Statement (UPS) from the pension provider of the current employer. The standardized layout of the UPSs made it easier to provide uniform consolidated online information.

Forced Transfers

Officials told us there are no forced transfers in the Netherlands. Rather, accounts that participants changing jobs do not transfer to a new plan stay in their old plan, but the annual indexation of benefits differ: inactive accounts are indexed to price inflation, whereas active accounts are indexed to wage inflation.

Pension Registry

The Netherlands launched the online pension registry in January 2011. The decision to establish the registry was part of the 2006 Pension Act.

Participant can see up-to-date pension information on active and also inactive accounts associated with previous employers, including account balances, account numbers and plan contact information. Active account information has to be mailed to participants on an annual basis and inactive account information every 5 years, according to Dutch officials. Recent data from the European Actuarial Consultative Group shows that the number of unique visitors to the registry was 1,500,000 in 2011 and 1,100,000 in 2012.

Pension providers, not the government, finance the pension registry at an annual cost of 2.3 million euro or .49 euro per active participant. Officials also said the cost of developing the pension registry was split between the pension fund industry and the insurance schemes industry, based on their share of the workplace retirement plan market. It took about 3 years and cost about 10 million euro to develop the new pension registry, according to Dutch government officials we interviewed.

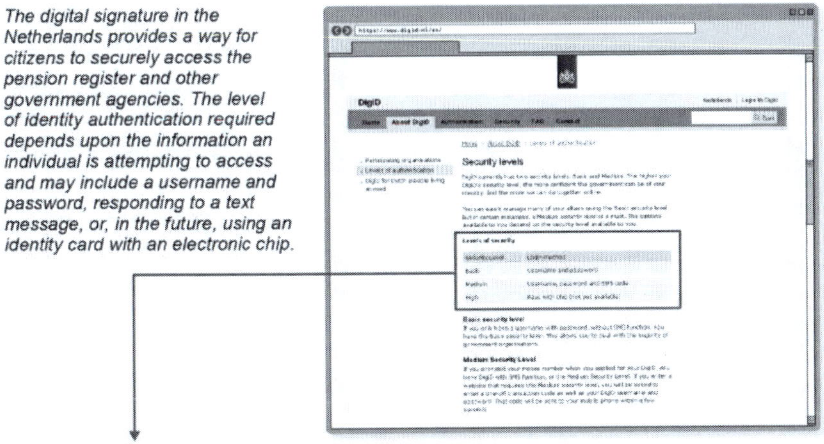

Levels of security

Security Level	Login method
Basic	Username and password
Medium	Username, password and SMS code
High	Pass with chip (not yet available)

Source: The Netherland's DigiID website (https://www.digid.nl/en/). | GAO-15-73.

Figure 16. Security Levels for the National Digital Signature.

Switzerland

At a Glance

The Swiss system is an example of how a retirement account can follow a participant as they move from job to job. Participants are required to transfer inactive workplace retirement accounts left with previous employers, according to Swiss government officials we interviewed. There are a variety of defined benefit and defined contribution plan types in Switzerland. As accounts move from plan to plan, conversion rules established in law govern the value of transferred assets.

Forced Transfers

The assets of inactive accounts in workplace plans are transferred to the Substitute Plan, which is a foundation, according to a Swiss insurer insuring 40 percent of the companies in Switzerland. There, they remain invested until the participant reaches retirement age or transfers the account to their active plan or vested benefits account, according to Swiss officials. At retirement age, officials at the institution providing plans insolvency insurance, the Guarantee Fund, contact participants and inform them of their forcibly-transferred account. The address these officials use is the address where participants receive their government (Social Security equivalent) retirement benefits. While plans must hold onto inactive accounts for at least 6 months after contributions have stopped, after 2 years, they must transfer them.

Pension Registry

There is no pension registry providing consolidated current online workplace retirement account information in Switzerland, according to Swiss government officials. Swiss Officials said when participants need information on a workplace retirement account started at a past employer, they refer to information provided by the employer or plan or contact the Guarantee Fund, which provides insolvency insurance to plans in Switzerland. Participants can contact officials at the Guarantee Fund by phone or e-mail to identify accounts that were forced out of their plan because they were inactive, according to Swiss officials and the Guarantee Fund's 2013 annual report.

Swiss officials said participants can use information on their inactive accounts to roll them over to the plan of their new employer. They said participants are required by Swiss law to transfer their retirement account when they change jobs, and because enrollment is generally mandatory, officials said employers will often help employees roll their money from their old plan to their new plan. Individuals without a new plan are required to purchase a vested benefit account at a bank or insurance company.

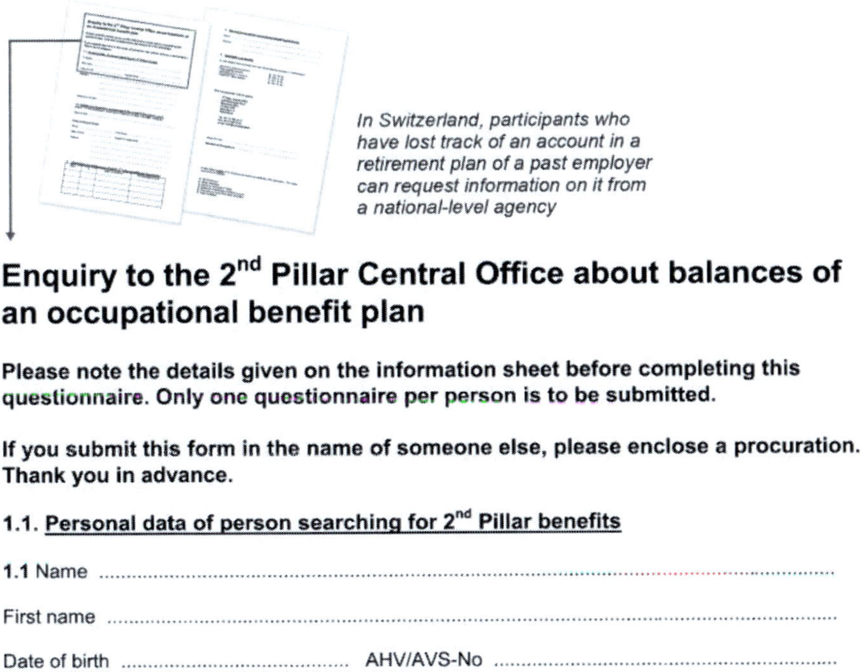
In Switzerland, participants who have lost track of an account in a retirement plan of a past employer can request information on it from a national-level agency

Enquiry to the 2nd Pillar Central Office about balances of an occupational benefit plan

Please note the details given on the information sheet before completing this questionnaire. Only one questionnaire per person is to be submitted.

If you submit this form in the name of someone else, please enclose a procuration. Thank you in advance.

1.1. Personal data of person searching for 2nd Pillar benefits

1.1 Name ....

First name ....

Date of birth .... AHV/AVS-No ....

Source: Swiss 2nd Pillar Central Office Website. | GAO-15-73.

Note: In Switzerland, participants who have lost track of an account in a retirement plan of a past employer can request information on it from a Swiss agency.

Figure 17. A Portion of a Swiss Form for Participants with Lost Accounts.

The United Kingdom

At a Glance

Parliament of the United Kingdom adopted The Pensions Act 2014 which will transfer small inactive workplace retirement accounts to an individual's active plan. Before the legislation, plans had ultimate discretion over whether or not to accept a transfer, according to a U.K. government report, and the onus for pursuing a transfer rested on individuals. Regulations will now be made to automatically transfer workplace retirement benefits, according to a U.K. official, preventing a plan from declining to accept such transfers. That process generally applies to defined contribution plans most U.K. participants are automatically enrolled in. Before the Pensions Act 2014, small, inactive retirement accounts were being reduced by fees and managed separately, and in an inefficient manner.

Forced Transfers

Once the Pensions Act 2014 is fully implemented, according to reports from the U.K. government, inactive 401(k)-type retirement accounts under £10,000 will be transferred into an account the employee actively contributes to by default if the employee does not opt out of the process. The legislation allows for the creation of a database to keep track transferrable accounts for that purpose.

Pension Registry

There is no pension registry in the United Kingdom providing direct access to consolidated retirement account information online, according to U.K. government officials. Individuals get information on lost accounts through a government service called the Pensions Tracing Service. Participants use the service to trace lost workplace or private retirement account based on information the participant supplies. The Pensions Tracing Service requests information from participants on their workplace or personal pension plan, such as names, addresses, dates of employment or participation in the plan, job title, and industry.

Individuals use the contact information of the plan administrator to determine their eligibility for retirement benefits, and if eligible, to claim them, according to a U.K. government research report. If the trace is successful, the Pensions Tracing Service provides the current name or contact details of the plan administrator to the individual. Participants can access the Pensions Tracing Service online, or by phone or mail.

The Pensions Tracing Service is a free service available to the general public in the United Kingdom provided by the U.K. Department for Work and Pensions.

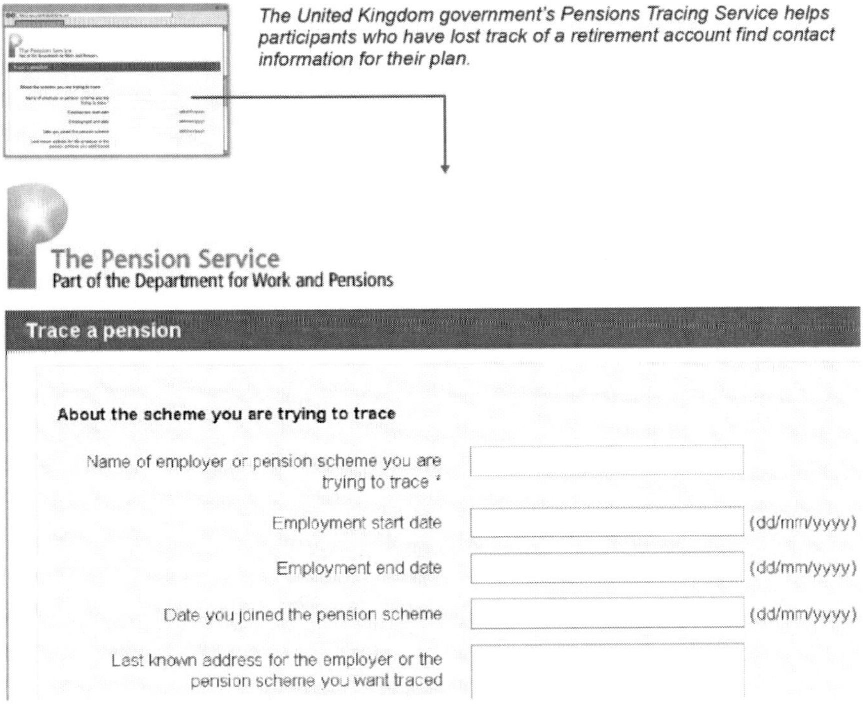

Source: Pension Tracing Service Website. | GAO-15-73.

Figure 18. Screenshot of a Pension Tracing Service Form.

End Notes

[1] In 2013, 38 percent of workers left their jobs. The average of the previous 5 years, 2008 to 2012, was a similar 38.4 percent. U.S. Bureau of Labor Statistics, Job Openings and Labor Turnover Survey, table 16.

[2] In this report, the term "plan" is used to mean a plan or plan sponsor under the Employee Retirement Income Security Act of 1974 (ERISA). Pub. L. No. 93-406, 88 Stat.829 (codified as amended at 29 U.S.C. §§ 1001-1461). Under ERISA, plans are sponsored by employers or employee organizations or jointly by both. Other countries use the terms "scheme" and "fund" in reference to workplace retirement benefits. We use the term plan when discussing workplace benefit provisions abroad and in the United States and when

referring to particular responsibilities that may technically fall to the plan sponsor or plan administrator.

[3] In this report, the term "savings" is used to mean the assets or funds in an individual's workplace retirement plan account and may include employee contributions, employer contributions, amounts attributable to rollovers from another plan or an IRA, and investment returns on any of these funds.

[4] In this report, the term "separated participant" includes those who left their job voluntarily or otherwise, retirees, and participants who kept their jobs but whose employer was bought out by another company.

[5] 26 U.S.C. §§ 401(a)(31) and 411(a)(11).

[6] Federal statute refers to this process as "mandatory distribution." 26 U.S.C. § 401(a)(31)(B). For this report, however, in the U.S. context, the term "forced transfer" is used. In an international context, the term "forced transfer" is used more broadly to mean the transfer of a participant's assets out of a retirement plan without their consent.

[7] Applicable Department of Labor (DOL) regulations use the term "automatic rollover" in connection with the use of these IRAs. 29 C.F.R. § 2550.404a-2(a). Those regulations also permit plans to purchase annuities for individuals forced out of plans, but our review did not include that option. In addition, IRA providers we interviewed did not indicate that annuities are used by plans seeking a destination for forced transfers.

[8] Federal statute permits plans to rollover accounts of more than $1,000 but not over $5,000 to an IRA on behalf of participants who have not instructed, for example, to have them rolled over to a new employer's plan or a pre-existing IRA, or sent directly to them. 26 U.S.C. § 401(a)(31)(B).

[9] In this report we use the term 'inactive' to refer to a retirement account where the account holder, a participant in a 401(k) plan, has changed jobs and is no longer making contributions. The account holder in such cases may or may not be 'missing' or otherwise not providing instruction, when requested, to the plan.

[10] In 2013, the Advisory Council on Employee Welfare and Pension Benefit Plans, also known as the ERISA Advisory Council, held 2 days of public hearings on June 4, 2013 and August 28, 2013 to hear testimony about "Lost Participant" issues from a number of constituencies. See *Advisory Council on Employee Welfare and Pension Benefit Plans, Locating Missing and Lost Participants*, (Washington, D.C.: November 2013).

[11] Pub. L. No. 107-16, 115 Stat. 38.

[12] § 657(a), 115 Stat. 135-36 (codified at 26 U.S.C. § 401(a)(31)(B)).This provision effectively codified a previous IRS ruling that a plan could make a direct rollover to an individual retirement plan (which is an IRA or an annuity) its default option for involuntary distributions, without jeopardizing its tax-qualified status, when a participant has a balance greater than $1,000 but not in excess of $5,000 and makes no election. Rev. Rul. 2000- 36, 2000-2 C.B. 140. We reviewed only the use of forced-transfer IRAs in this report. EGTRRA also provided that plan amounts may be determined for such purposes without regard to any portion of a participant's account attributable to rollovers and their earnings. § 648, 115 Stat. 127 (codified at 26 U.S.C. § 411(a)(11)(D)).

[13] 26 U.S.C. § 411(a)(11).

[14] Pub. L. No. 107-16, § 657(c)(2)(A), 115 Stat. 38, 136.

[15] Fiduciary Responsibility Under the Employee Retirement Income Security Act of 1974 Automatic Rollover Safe Harbor, 69 Fed. Reg. 58,018 (Sept. 28, 2004) (codified at 29 C.F.R. § 2550.404a-2).

[16] The safe harbor ensures that both (1) a plan administrator's designation of an institution to receive the forced-transfer, and (2) the initial investment choice for the rolled-over funds will be deemed to satisfy ERISA's fiduciary standard of care at 29 U.S.C. § 1104(a). In addition, a financial institution may designate itself or an affiliate to receive the forced-transfers from its own plan, and select a proprietary initial investment for the funds, under the terms of a prohibited transaction exemption developed in conjunction with the safe harbor. 29 U.S.C. § 1106 and Class Exemption for the Establishment, Investment and Maintenance of Certain Individual Retirement Plans Pursuant to a Mandatory Distribution, 69 Fed. Reg. 57,964 (Sept. 28, 2004).

[17] If a participant's account is $1,000 or less, a plan can complete a forced transfer by paying the account balance directly to the participant, which is a taxable event. The plan would withhold 20 percent of the balance for possible tax liability. An additional 10 percent tax may apply if the individual is under age 59 1/2 at the time of the distribution. 26 U.S.C. § 72(t).

[18] Plan Sponsor Council of America's (PSCA) *55th Annual Survey of Profit Sharing and 401(k) Plans*. Another 42 percent simply cash out balances less than $1,000 and let larger balances remain in the plan, while just 7 percent allow balances of any size to remain in the plan after a participant separates. The survey collects data on the 2011 plan experience from 840 plans with more than 10 million participants and more than $750 billion in plan assets. PSCA surveys both profit sharing plans and 401(k) plans. Some of the data we use from this report are for only 401(k) plans, but other data are for both kinds of plans combined. Given that just 2 percent of plans surveyed are profit sharing plans, we determined the data are sufficiently representative of the 401(k) plan experience. There are no comprehensive federal or private industry data on the number of forced-transfer IRAs created or the amount of employer-based retirement savings transferred into them.

[19] SSA analysis of Form 8955-SSA data, which are collected by IRS and then transmitted to SSA. SSA data include benefits left behind by separating participants in all defined contribution plans, including 401(k) plans, as well as in defined benefit plans, which are not subject to forced transfers under 26 U.S.C. § 401(a)(31)(B). GAO assessed the reliability of the data and found that it met our standards for our purposes.

[20] While forced-transfer IRA providers could invest money in assets other than money market funds, certificates of deposit, or savings accounts, such investments would not meet DOL's current requirements for the safe harbor.

[21] 29 C.F.R. § 2550.404a-2(c)(3)(ii).

[22] 29 C.F.R. § 2550.404a-2(c)(3).

[23] Data are from Morningstar.com.

[24] When we refer to returns, we mean the fund return net of fund investment expenses. We found that the fund return is generally equivalent to the return for the account because all but one IRA provider we interviewed use only one default investment per account. When we refer to fees, we mean additional fees charged by the provider generally expressed as dollar amounts.

[25] This reflects one provider's policy of charging a 20 percent opening fee for a "premium" forced-transfer IRA account, which must have a balance of at least $500.

[26] Administrative fees paid on a forced-transfer IRA include account opening fees, address search fees for a missing account holder, and annual administrative fees. An account holder might also pay transaction fees and account closure fees if they decide to reinvest or transfer the savings in their forced-transfer IRA.

[27] We used a $1,000 starting balance to simplify the observation of the effect. While most balances declined over time, two gained slightly in value and one had no change in value—after an initial decrease due to the account opening fee—because fees are capped at the value of the investment returns.

[28] This projection reflects one forced-transfer IRA's $50 account set-up fee, a recurring $50 annual fee, and a recurring $65 annual address search fee, with a 0.11 percent investment return. The same provider uses three other default investments, which would also contribute to the balance decreasing to $0 in 9 years. See appendix III for all forced-transfer IRA combinations that we analyzed.

[29] This reflects adding the annual decrease on a $1,000 balance (7.3 percent) attributable to the median account opening fee of $6.75 and the median annual fee of $42 and the average annual inflation rate over 20 years from 1993 to 2013 (2.45 percent), according to the U.S. Bureau of Labor Statistics' Consumer Price Index for All Urban Consumers (CPI-U).

[30] Target date funds are designed to be long-term investments for individuals with particular retirement dates in mind. For more information on target date funds, see GAO, *Defined Contribution Plans: Key Information on Target Date Funds as Default Investments Should Be Provided to Plan Sponsors and Participants*, GAO-11-118 (Washington, D.C.: Jan. 31, 2011).

[31] Morningstar.com, Morningstar Fund Research Target-Date Series Research Paper: Survey 2013, p.20. The paper reports that "[f]rom the pre-crisis peak in 2007 through the end of 2012, all but one of the currently extant 2015 funds have recouped their losses, and most have produced double digit positive gains."

[32] The mean total return for taxable money market fund investments over 10 years ending July 31, 2014 was 1.45 percent, whereas the geometric mean of 10-year returns for all target date funds was 6.3 percent, according to our analysis of data from Morningstar.com. Money market funds, such as those commonly used in forced-transfer IRAs, have not always underperformed target date funds common to 401(k) plans. In 2008, during the last recession, 2010 target date funds had a negative total net return in the double digits while money market funds overall earned a return of 2.05 percent. Still, equities-based funds like target date funds are designed to perform well over the long run.

[33] DOL's qualified default investment alternative regulation provides relief to plan fiduciaries who comply with notice and other requirements when investing on behalf of plan participants who fail to direct their own investments. 29 C.F.R. § 2550.404c-5. It includes three categories of investments that may be eligible as qualified default investment alternatives—target date or similar funds, balanced funds, and managed accounts.

[34] 26 U.S.C. §§ 401(a)(31)(B)(i) and 7701(a)(37). We reviewed only the use of forced-transfer IRAs in this report, and providers we interviewed did not indicate that individual retirement annuities are used by plans seeking a destination for forced transfers.

[35] The specific investment products held in IRAs and 401(k) plans, as well as the various financial professionals that service them, are subject to oversight from applicable securities, banking, or insurance regulators, which can include both federal and state regulators.

[36] Generally, DOL has interpretive jurisdiction over prohibited transactions and IRS has certain enforcement authority. See GAO, *Individual Retirement Accounts: Government Actions Could Encourage More Employers to Offer IRAs to Employees,* GAO-08-590 (Washington, D.C.: June 4, 2008).

[37] 26 U.S.C. § 4975 and 29 U.S.C. § 1108. Terminating plans force out both current and separated participants' balances to dispose of all plan assets, as required to complete a plan termination.

[38] Officials at PBGC told us that they are in the process of expanding their existing program, which takes custody of and invests pension assets of terminated defined benefit plans to include this new role. PBGC hopes to open its program to terminating defined contribution plans in 2016.

[39] In the future, additional alternatives to the forced-transfer IRA may be available, such as the forthcoming "My Retirement Account" (myRA), which is to be initially offered through employers.

[40] 26 U.S.C. § 411(a)(11)(D). Amounts rolled over into a new plan from another workplace plan remain vested in the new plan, although they do not count toward the vested balance for purposes of determining eligibility for forced transfer once a participant has separated from the plan.

[41] For example, some plans offer investment choices with fees that reflect the lower pricing available for institutional grade shares. A fund's "institutional" class of shares are generally available only to investors of large sums, such as a pension fund or a trust for a university, and are less expensive than share classes available to an individual retail investor. GAO, *401(k) Plans: Labor and IRS Could Improve the Rollover Process for Participants*, GAO-13-30 (Washington, D.C.: Mar. 7, 2013).

[42] We chose the service sector for our projections because more than half of defined contribution plans (like 401(k) plans) are in the service sector and about 40 percent of defined contribution plan participants, according to a 2011 report by the Employee Benefits Security Administration. The annual salary data used for our projections are for the food preparation- and serving-related occupations.

[43] Our assumptions include plan service requirements, deferral rates, employer-matching rates, and vesting, among other factors. All our projections assumed a plan investment in a target date fund, the most common default investment for automatic enrollment, with a return of 6.30 percent, the geometric mean of 10-year average returns for all target date funds ending July 31, 2014, based on GAO analysis of data from Morningstar.com. See appendix IV to see all projections and assumptions used.

[44] By statute, any such service requirement may extend no longer than the later of the date on which an employee attains the age of 21 or completes 1 year of service. 26 U.S.C. § 410(a)(1)(A).

[45] PSCA's 55th *Annual Survey of Profit Sharing and 401(k) Plans*, (Reflecting the 2011 Plan Experience), table 11.

[46] Data are from the U.S. Bureau of Labor Statistics for both men and women in January 2012. http://data.bls.gov/cgi-bin/print.pl/news.release/tenure

[47] SSA analysis of Form 8955-SSA data. SSA data include benefits left behind by separating participants in all defined contribution plans, including 401(k) plans, as well as in defined benefit plans, which are not subject to forced transfers. GAO assessed the reliability of the data and found that it met our standards for our purposes.

[48] GAO-13-30. Plans are not currently required to accept rollovers. One issue that plans have with accepting rollovers is with verifying that funds coming from outside a plan are legally tax qualified under the Internal Revenue Code. We previously recommended that IRS and DOL work together to communicate to plan sponsors IRS's guidance on the relief from tax disqualification provided for plans that accept rollovers later determined to have come from a plan that was not tax qualified. Subsequently, on April 3, 2014, IRS issued guidance to ease the process and make plan-to-plan rollovers less burdensome for plans. The ruling provides a simple method for receiving plans to verify the tax-qualified status of sending

plans by checking a recent annual report (Form 5500) filing for the sending plan on a public database. Rev. Rul. 2014-9, 2014-7 I.R.B. 975.

[49] 29 C.F.R. § 2250.401a-2(c)(4).

[50] GAO, *Retirement Savings: Automatic Enrollment Shows Promise for Some Workers, but Proposals to Broaden Retirement Savings for Other Workers Could Face Challenges*, GAO-10-31 (Washington, D.C.: Oct. 23, 2009).

[51] U.S. Dept. of Labor, Field Assistance Bulletin 2014-01 (Aug.14, 2014).

[52] GAO, *Private Pensions: Clarity of Required Reports and Disclosures Could Be Improved*, GAO-14-92, (Washington, D.C., Nov. 21, 2013).

[53] GAO-14-92.

[54] 29 U.S.C. § 1023. The Form 5500 Series Report is the primary source of information for both the federal government and the private sector regarding the operation, funding, assets, and investments of private pension plans and other employee benefit plans. DOL, IRS, and PBGC jointly developed the Form 5500 so employee benefit plans could satisfy annual reporting requirements under ERISA and the IRC.

[55] For a more complete description of plan reporting and disclosure requirements, see GAO-14-92.

[56] In addition, DOL officials told us that employer identification numbers are often reported incorrectly. Questions on the Form 5500, 5500-SF, and schedules H and I require sponsors to provide information on plan termination and transfers to other plans.

[57] GAO-14-92.

[58] If the Notice is regarding a defined benefit plan it will include information about the estimated benefit due to the participant at the time that they separated from their employer.

[59] According to SSA, individuals who apply for Title II disability benefits will receive the Notice at the time of filing that application, which may be earlier than age 62.

[60] Advertising efforts can be effective in routing an interested public toward otherwise underused federal resources and websites. Officials at PBGC told us that when one retiree advocacy organization published information about PBGC's registry of lost accounts the agency saw a surge in online hits to the registry.

[61] 42 U.S.C. § 1320b-13. The Statement also explains how benefits are estimated. See GAO, *Social Security Statements: Observations on SSA's Plans for the Social Security Statement*, GAO-11-787T, (Washington, D.C., July 8, 2011). The earnings history shows an individual's income subject to Social Security tax. Not all earnings are subject to Social Security tax. The law also requires each statement to contain the following: an estimate of the potential monthly Social Security retirement, disability, survivor, and auxiliary benefits and a description of the benefits under Medicare; and the amount of wages paid to the employee and income from self-employment, among other things.

[62] The mailings will be sent to workers aged 25, 30, 35, 40, 45, 50, 55, 60, or older, who have not created an online account with SSA.

[63] A service bus is technology that manages access to applications and services to present a simple, consistent interface to end users online.

[64] To contact retirees, the Swiss use the address where retirees receive their public pension, much like SSA sends U.S. retirees a Potential Private Retirement Benefit Information notice.

[65] Officials said while these transfers move accounts without affirmative participant consent, if participants explicitly request that their account not follow them from job to job, they are permitted to opt-out of the process and leave their account behind in their previous employer's plan.

[66] Although regulations implementing the 2014 Pensions Act are not final, the U.K. Department for Work and Pensions consulted with stakeholders who suggested that once an individual leaves a job, that employer might upload information about their account there to a database. The employee's new employer would search the database for details of the old account, inform the individual of the transfer process, and if the employee does not opt-out, contact the employee's old plan to request the transfer. Stakeholders thought that a combination of full name, National Insurance Number, and date of birth could be used to successfully match members with their accounts in the United Kingdom.

[67] To learn of industry efforts in the United States to help plan accounts follow participants, we spoke with a forced-transfer IRA provider who markets itself as a clearinghouse that will find the participant and their current plan, and consolidate their forced-transfer into it. The forced-transfer IRA provider has used data from service providers to identify participants' current plans, and has successfully transferred thousands of accounts to the current plans of participants.

[68] The amount of interest paid, which has been equal to inflation since July 1st 2013, is set by regulation.

[69] While the Belgian pension registry is not scheduled to be operational for participants until 2016, plans already have some access to the data.

[70] A representative of a plan in Belgium said the plan shares each participant's terms of benefit contract with the pension registry. As a result, an individual who disagrees with their retirement benefit has the opportunity to access the actual contract, which, according to one Belgian plan, resolves the vast majority of disputes.

[71] Providing the functionality to view and analyze such comprehensive information in the United States could overlap with private sector financial planning tools which analyze information provided by individuals.

[72] The pension registry (PensionsInfo) in Denmark did not require legislation. Danish University Professors said initial discussions centered on leading people to an understanding of their retirement benefits, but to understand them, people had to know what they were.

[73] According to European Commission officials, the Netherlands, Latvia, Bulgaria, France, and Austria all provide part consolidated online retirement account information to participants on a secure website. In addition to the one in Denmark, European Commission officials said pension registries in Sweden, Finland, and Norway also analyzed the data for participants for financial planning purposes.

[74] According to PBGC officials, the agency is working with DOL and IRS to develop a proposal to implement the expansion.

End Notes for Appendix I

[1] In 2013, the Advisory Council on Employee Welfare and Pension Benefit Plans, also known as the ERISA Advisory Council, held 2 days of public hearings on June 4, 2013, and August 28, 2013, to hear testimony about "Lost Participant" Issues from a number of constituencies. See *Advisory Council on Employee Welfare and Pension Benefit Plans, Locating Missing and Lost Participants*, (Washington, D.C.: November 2013).

[2] As described in the report, plans must transfer forced out balances of $1,000-$5,000 to forced-transfer IRAs and have the option, but are not required, to transfer smaller forced-out balances into forced-transfer IRAs.

End Notes for Appendix II

[1] We asked PLANSPONSOR.com to include questions about plan sponsors' use of forced transfers in its newsletter, which is distributed to online subscribers. Respondents to the query included 14 plan sponsors and 4 third-party administrators/record keepers.

[2] When a plan issues a distribution check, either at the request of the separated participant or after the forced transfer of a participant with a balance below $1,000 when the participant has given no instructions, the check often remains uncashed. The funds represented by uncashed checks could be very significant. Several industry professionals have estimated that uncashed distribution checks may represent billions in retirement savings. Checks may remain uncashed because the mailing address is out of date and the check is undeliverable or the recipient either forgets or opts not to cash the check. Uncashed checks leave plans in a difficult and ambiguous position. By transferring balances to a forced-transfer IRA, plans can complete the forced-transfer of participants with these small accounts and conclude their relationship to the former participant consistent with their fiduciary standard of care. Some plans that would like to use forced-transfer IRAs for this purpose may have difficulty finding a provider willing to accept balances under $1,000, perhaps because—as indicated by several providers we interviewed—providing the accounts is not very profitable. However, for some force-out IRA providers, filling this gap in service by providing force-out IRAs for small balances is part of their business model. Two providers we interviewed accept transfers down to $1.

[3] 26 U.S.C. 401(a)(31)(B)(i) and IRS Notice 2005-5, 2015-1 C.B. 337.

[4] While there is no stated regulatory requirement, prudence under section 404(a) of ERISA dictates that a plan search for participants before distributing benefits when it is known that a participant is missing, e.g., the plan receives a returned 402(f) notice or other disclosure notice. Plans could use the search steps in FAB 2014-01 for terminating plans as a guide to searching for missing participants in ongoing plans.

[5] Among the forced-transfer IRA provider data we reviewed, the median annual fee was $42, although the highest was $115 plus a small percentage of assets. Annual fees sometimes include address search services, but sometimes extra search fees are applied to the account.

[6] PSCA's *55th Annual Survey of Profit Sharing and 401(k) Plans*. Another 42 percent simply cash out balances less than $1,000 and let larger balances remain in the plan, while 7 percent allow balances of any size to remain in the plan after a participant separates. There are no comprehensive federal or private industry data on the number of forced-transfer IRAs created or the amount of employer-based retirement savings transferred into them.

[7] One provider did not provide the number and value of accounts opened, so these totals reflect data for 9 of the 10 companies for which we collected account fee and return data.

[8] SSA analysis of Form 8955-SSA data. SSA data include vested benefits in all defined contribution plans, not just those from 401(k) plans, as well as defined benefit plans. We previously reported that data from the form 8955-SSA on potential benefits that retirees may be owed by former employers are not always updated or verified over time. GAO, *Private Pensions: Clarity of Required Reports and Disclosures Could be Improved*, GAO-14-92 (Washington, D.C., Nov. 21, 2013). Because defined benefit plans do not use forced transfers, those accounts are not subject to these rules. We determined that the data provided were reliable for our purposes.

[9] Accounts of less than $1,000 could also be transferred to IRAs, absent participant instruction.

[10] We identified the largest forced-transfer IRA provider among those we interviewed based on total forced-transfer IRAs under management. We identified forced-transfer IRA providers

through interviews with experts, government officials, other forced-transfer IRA and general IRA providers, and a literature review.

[11] Plans cannot use forced-transfer IRAs unless their summary plan description or a summary of material modifications to the plan reflects such a policy and communicates it to plan participants as prescribed by regulation. 29 C.F.R. § 2550.404a-2(c)(4).

[12] PSCA's *55th Annual Survey of Profit Sharing and 401(k) Plans*, table 132, "Pre-retirement distributions options offered." Data reflect 2011 plan experiences.

[13] The forced-transfer IRA accounts are not profitable for the company so they only offer them as a service to ongoing clients with an active plan looking to transfer eligible balances.

[14] U.S. Dept. of Labor, Field Assistance Bulletin 2014-01 (Aug. 14, 2014).

In: 401(k) Plans
Editor: Suzanne Abbott
ISBN: 978-1-63482-598-6

Chapter 2

LOCATING MISSING AND LOST PARTICIPANTS*

Advisory Council on Employee Welfare and Pension Benefit Plans

ABSTRACT

The 2013 ERISA Advisory Council ("Council") examined the issues plan sponsors, fiduciaries, service providers, and other parties ("Plan Representatives") face in handling plan benefits payable to participants and beneficiaries who cannot be found or are nonresponsive ("Lost Participants"). The focus of the Council's examination was on both methods of maintaining contact with participants so they do not become Lost Participants and methods of finding participants once they become Lost Participants.

The Council learned from witnesses who testified that locating Lost Participants to pay them their benefits can be an administrative burden. Further, while there is DOL guidance on dealing with Lost Participants, that guidance is (i) focused on terminated defined contribution plans, (ii) presented in multiple sources rather than one central and cohesive resource, or (iii) outdated. Furthermore, there does not appear to be sufficient inter-agency coordination among the DOL, the Pension Benefit Guaranty Corporation, and the Social Security Administration to address

* This is an edited, reformatted and augmented version of a report to the Honorable Thomas E. Perez, United States Secretary of Labor, issued November 2013.

overlapping issues surrounding Lost Participants. The Council makes several recommendations in this report regarding how to address each of these findings.

I. EXECUTIVE SUMMARY

The 2013 ERISA Advisory Council ("Council") examined issues that plan sponsors, fiduciaries, service providers, and other parties ("Plan Representatives") face in handling plan benefits payable to participants and beneficiaries who cannot be found or are nonresponsive ("Lost Participants"). The Council focused on methods of maintaining contact with participants so they do not become Lost Participants and methods of finding participants once they become Lost Participants.

Plans of all sizes deal with the challenge of finding Lost Participants. The challenges are particularly great in large plans and industries with high employee turnover or a large number of seasonal employees. While the dollar amount of any single Lost Participant's benefit is typically small, the aggregate dollar amounts across all participants and beneficiaries can be large. Further, plan service providers often are in a position where they have many uncashed benefits checks attributable to many different plans across their customer base.

Closely connected to the Lost Participant issue is the problem of "lost pensions," which most often arises in the case of legacy defined benefit plans. As time goes by and plan sponsors change or plans are merged into other plans, retirees can lose track of the plans in which they participated. The Council heard testimony that participants and beneficiaries might be losing out on their pensions due to shortcomings in the retirement system whereby plan sponsors, plans and retirees lose contact with each other over the years. Many of the Council's recommendations are designed to help participants maintain closer contact with their benefits and also would help address the lost pension problem.

The Council heard witnesses from a variety of constituencies impacted by Lost Participant issues, including: plan sponsors, retiree advocacy groups, services providers, accountants, policy organizations, and related trade associations. The Council also heard testimony from representatives of governmental agencies including DOL, the Social Security Administration ("SSA") and the Pension Benefit Guaranty Corporation ("PBGC"). Testimony occurred during two days of public hearings held on June 4, 2013 and August 28, 2013.

Based upon this testimony and other information submitted to the Council, the Council formulated several recommendations focused on the DOL taking action in three areas: (i) developing industry best practices, (ii) updating and supplementing guidance addressing Lost Participant issues, and (iii) working with other governmental agencies to create a coordinated approach to addressing Lost Participant issues.

II. RECOMMENDATIONS

The Council recommends that the DOL take actions in three areas – development of best practices, additional legal guidance, and coordination with other government agencies.

A. Industry Best Practices
  1. Develop and maintain suggestions for plan sponsors, plan administrators, plan fiduciaries and service providers for improving administrative practices in the following areas:
    a) keeping track of participants before they become lost;
    b) providing information to participants on the importance of keeping contact information up to date, providing alternate contacts that can be used when the participant is not responsive, and reminders to verify and update this information -- such as call center or web login reminders and plan benefit statements reminders;
    c) providing information to participants about the opportunity to consolidate assets through rollover to the current employer's plan or an IRA; and
    d) effective search methods for locating Lost Participants, including use of web search and commercial locator services.

B. Legal Guidance on Fiduciary and Other Issues
  1. Update guidance for terminated plans under FAB 2004-02 or issue other guidance to provide or clarify the following:
    a) search options other than governmental locator programs (e.g., cost effective commercial locator services and other search vehicles) are appropriate under ERISA and should be accorded safe harbor status under ERISA, with a menu of approaches being acceptable;

b) if the Pension Benefit Guaranty Corporation implements a lost participant program for terminated DC plans, compliance with the program also should be accorded safe harbor status under ERISA; and

c) the guidance applies to both participants and beneficiaries.

2. Issue guidance addressing plan fiduciary obligations to locate missing and nonresponsive participants and beneficiaries in active and frozen defined contribution plans that parallels the guidance for terminated plans in FAB 2004- 02. Such guidance should:

a) Consolidate DOL's prior guidance in this area;

b) confirm that a plan may provide that the distribution amount of an uncashed benefit check may be returned to the plan's forfeiture account if a reasonable effort has been made to reach the participant/beneficiary; provided that the benefit (without earnings) will be restored if and when the participant or beneficiary claims the benefit;

c) allow a plan to presume that a participant/beneficiary who fails to cash a benefit check after a specified period of time may be treated as a lost participant/beneficiary; and

d) provide guidance on charging search costs to participant/ beneficiary accounts, including the handling of small accounts where search costs may exceed the account value.

3. Extend the automatic rollover provisions in the safe harbor under DOL Regulation section 2550.404a-2 to:

a) Lost Participants, including those who fail to cash benefit checks (regardless of the size of the account) that become payable to the participant upon attainment of the plan's normal retirement age or are otherwise distributable without the participant consent under Code Sec. 411 and the terms of the plan; and

b) Lost beneficiaries (regardless of the size of the account or timing of the distribution).

4. Issue updated guidance on ERISA preemption of state abandoned property laws with respect to Lost Participants.

5. Issue guidance to clarify the status of assets used to satisfy benefit payment obligations while a benefit check remains uncashed, including:

a) whether or not the uncashed checks and underlying amounts are plan assets;

b) the appropriate accounting treatment for such, including monitoring and internal controls; and
c) the appropriate reporting and disclosure requirements in the annual filing of the Form 5500.

C. Developing an Integrated Regulatory Regime
1. Work with other federal agencies with respect to programs aimed at Lost Participants, including suggestions and support for the following:
a) Enhance the current reporting system for information on terminated vested participants under Code section 6057;
b) Enhance the form letter, entitled "Potential Private Retirement Benefit Information," sent to terminated vested participants by the Social Security Administration, to include references to relevant agency publications and websites with information on lost participants;
c) Develop and implement the Pension Benefit Guaranty Corporation program for Lost Participants under ERISA section 4050 and establish a national plan registry; and
d) Promote federally funded pension counseling projects, such as including website links on relevant agency websites to the "Finding a Lost Pension" booklet.

III. COUNCIL'S REVIEW OF LOST PARTICIPANT ISSUES

The Council heard testimony that covered a wide range of issues involving Lost Participants. However, a number of common themes emerged from the testimony that formed the basis for recommendations in three distinct areas. The Council's recommendations and this discussion are organized around the following broad major areas:

1) Industry Best Practices;
2) Legal Guidance on Fiduciary and Other Issues; and
3) Developing an Integrated Regulatory Regime.

Each of these areas is addressed in subsections A, B, and C below. At the end of each section, the Council made several observations that led to the recommendations in Section II of this paper.

In summary, the Council believes that there are straightforward steps that plans, participants and governmental agencies can take to ensure that participants remain connected with their benefits. For plans, the steps include maintaining and updating contact information and prompt searches for participants when the contact information is no longer valid. For participants, the steps include being responsible for keeping plans informed of their contact information or consolidating assets in their new employer's plan or an IRA. The government steps include DOL guidance on plan sponsor responsibilities with respect to Lost Participants and better coordination of DOL, PBGC and SSA programs designed to ensure that benefits are paid as intended.

The Council wishes to thank all of the witnesses for their insights and perspectives on the subject of Lost Participant issues. The breadth and depth of the testimony and expertise has contributed immeasurably to this report.

A. Industry Best Practices

The Council heard testimony from a variety of constituencies (employer, service provider, etc.) to get a better understanding of how Lost Participant issues are addressed in the marketplace. In this subsection, the Council grouped the testimony it received regarding industry practices into what the Council hopes will serve as a framework for the formulation of industry "best practices" that may be employed by Plan Representatives.

1. Methods for Minimizing the Occurrence of Lost Participants

Many of the witnesses testified that they implemented procedures designed to minimize the occurrence of Lost Participants. They also emphasized the importance of the participants' and beneficiaries' roles in assuring that the Plan Representatives are able to communicate with them, even after termination from employment. Some of the procedures presented to the Council are summarized below.

"Scrub" Data

In testimony by J. Spencer Williams, on behalf of Retirement Clearinghouse, Mr. Spencer indicated that "the best solution is one that keeps participant data as up-to-date as practical, with the least cost and with minimal manual intervention." He suggested that employers or service providers periodically "scrub" their participant data to determine which participants have inaccurate information. Rob Martorano, National Defined Benefit Practice Leader for Aon Hewitt, and Mary Steigerwalt of Risk Compliance Performance Solutions made similar recommendations.

A "scrubbing" of data generally involves the comparison of an electronic data file pulled from the plan's recordkeeping system to another source of data. The National Change of Address ("NCOA") database created by the U.S. Postal service is a common database for such comparisons. Also, for purposes of locating beneficiaries, plan data may be compared to the Social Security Administration Death Index. Ideally, the scrubbing process results in identifying differences in addresses between the plan records and these databases. Plan sponsors or service providers, like Aon Hewitt and Retirement Clearinghouse, then send postcards or some other confirmation mailing to determine if the address acquired from the database is valid. Opinions regarding how often the "scrubbing" should occur vary. The general consensus among the witnesses was at least annually, but Mr. Williams thought quarterly would be more effective. Aon Hewitt recommends a data scrub two times per year. The cost of "scrubbing" is very low and could be as little as thirty-five cents per participant, but the cost varies by the company that performs such services. As part of its Lost Participant service, AON Hewitt also creates an audit report designed to demonstrate the steps taken to identify and locate the Lost Participants. Mr. Martorano indicated this might be helpful in demonstrating compliance with ERISA's prudence requirements.

Maintain Multiple Points of Contact

Several witnesses highlighted the importance of providing alternate points or methods of contact in the event a participant is not responsive. Mr. Martorano stated that AON Hewitt, which is a record keeper, is able to maintain on behalf of its plan clients a variety of contact information. Ms. Vicki Blanton, Senior Benefits Counsel for American Airlines, Inc., testifying on behalf of the American Benefits Council ("ABC"), also noted that her employer maintains multiple addresses. Alternate points of contact may include a participant's home address, beneficiary's home address, alternate addresses (e.g., participant second homes), multiple phone numbers (e.g., home, work, and cell) for participants and beneficiaries, and multiple e-mail addresses (e.g., work and personal) for participants and beneficiaries. Importantly, the point of maintaining this type of information is not to send plan-related information to every address. Rather, such information would be sent to the primary address on the plan's records. However, the additional information may help ease the burden of locating the Lost Participant once the primary address proves to be invalid or a participant or beneficiary is nonresponsive (e.g., fails to cash a benefit check).

Regularly Update Contact Information

According to several witnesses, many Plan Representatives use their regular interactions with participants and beneficiaries in the normal course of running the plan to remind participants and beneficiaries to update contact information. Further, the Council learned that plan sponsors often communicate to their participants and beneficiaries that it is their responsibility to update the Plan Representative when contact information changes. One plan sponsor even makes that obligation clear in the plan document.

The Council heard testimony that many plan sponsors utilize their call centers to validate the participant's contact information on file such as address, phone number, and email. Mr. Thomas Emswiler, Director of Participant Operations and Policy at the Federal Retirement Thrift Investment Board, pointed to a very thorough process that the Thrift Savings Plan ("TSP") uses to minimize the occurrence of Lost Participants. The TSP flags a participant's account when an incorrect address is identified through the NCOA database. In the event that the participant calls the TSP's call center, service representatives see the flag and ask the participant to update his or her address. Aon Hewitt similarly flags participant accounts on its recordkeeping system. In addition, if a participant logs on to his account electronically, the participant will be asked to update his or her information. Ms. Allison Klausner, Honeywell, also testifying on behalf of ABC, confirmed the effectiveness of using the log-on process to update account information.

Ms. Klausner and Ms. Blanton also pointed to the printed benefit statement as a place to remind participants to verify contact information and to update as needed. Ms. Jane Smith of the Pension Rights Center even recommended that the DOL regulation governing participant account statements and notices of vested benefits require warnings to participants to maintain records and to stay in touch with their retirement plan. Finally, the TSP and Aon Hewitt often call participants once they are aware of a bad address or a participant has proven to be nonresponsive.

Provide Information about the Consolidation of Multiple Account Balances

Providing participants with information about the opportunity to consolidate multiple plan account balances through the rollover process may help reduce the number of Lost Participants. According to Mr. Williams, one of the major causes of Lost Participants is frequent job changing. In addition, employees change their residences several times throughout their lifetimes. Ms. Klausner also pointed to the nature of today's workforce as a contributing factor. As a result, employees participate in multiple defined contribution plans and they lose track of their accumulated benefits. As a result, contact information is not updated and a Lost Participant issue eventually arises. Often, participants leave their account with a prior employer because they are satisfied with the investment choices. However, in other circumstances, participants may not be aware that they have one or more account balances or that they could rollover their account balances into their new plan or an IRA.

Mr. Williams stated that "widespread adoption of 'automatic,' systematic and timely plan-to plan roll-ins would...address the root cause of system friction, and eliminate 90 95% of the volume of lost and missing participants, and at the same time dramatically reduce cash outs and simplify management of their retirement savings for millions of Americans." Ms. Klausner stated that providing information about the rollover process could be helpful, but cautioned against going so far as to giving "advice," which the DOL will view as a fiduciary act.

2. Searching for Lost Participants

Once a determination is made by a Plan Representative that a participant or beneficiary is "lost," Plan Representatives often make some effort to search for the Lost Participants. There does not appear to be a common understanding as to when or if a participant or beneficiary might be characterized as "missing" or "lost." However, at least one witness testified that a participant or beneficiary was identified as "lost" when he or she is due a benefit and notices sent regarding the benefit are returned as undeliverable or he or she is unresponsive. In other cases, a Plan Representative may make this determination earlier such as when a plan disclosure (e.g., plan notices, qualified default investment alternative notices, etc.) are returned by the U.S. Post Office as undeliverable. In any event, the Plan Representative will eventually determine that a Lost Participant issue has arisen and determine whether action must be taken. The witnesses told the Council about a number of ways a Plan Representative may conduct a search and related issues.

Tiered Approach to Search Methods

The Council heard testimony regarding effective procedures for locating Lost Participants. The witnesses from the Retirement Clearinghouse and Risk Compliance Performance Solutions (both companies that provide Lost Participant search services) described a methodical, tiered approach to performing searches. At each tier, the search process becomes less automated, but the level of detail involved in the search (and the cost) correspondingly increases. An example of a tiered search approach could look like the following:

1. Compare the plan's records related to the Lost Participants to the NCOA database. To the extent there is a conflict of addresses, an address confirmation is sent to the new address or both addresses.
2. Use a credit reporting bureaus (e.g., Experian, Equifax, and TransUnion).
3. Use a commercial locator service (e.g., LexisNexis).
4. Perform manual searches using popular search engines (e.g., Bing, Google, etc.) or even industry specific databases (e.g., IMBD).

Richard McHugh, partner at Porter Wright Morris & Arthur LLP testifying for the Plan Sponsor Council of America ("PSCA"), also described search methods that reflect those set forth in DOL Field Assistance Bulletin 2004-2, which is summarized in the next section. In the event a participant or beneficiary cannot be located after sending a notice by regular mail, the Plan Representative often will do the following:

1. Send a notice to the most recent address on the Plan's records using certified-return receipt mail.
2. Check the records of other employer-sponsored plans (e.g.. health insurance, life insurance, defined benefit plan) to find more current information.
3. Identify and contact the participant's named beneficiary or contingent beneficiary.
4. Use a commercial locator service or a government letter forwarding service.

Mr. Martarano described a Lost Participant search service in which Aon Hewitt partnered with Risk Compliance Performance Solutions ("RCPS") in order to provide a Lost Participant locator service to its clients. That service also provides for different levels of search. For example, Ms. Steigerwalt noted that RCPS experienced considerable success using LexisNexis to find the phone numbers of plan participants. RCPS then called the Lost Participants in order to get new contact information.

One or more of the steps described above may be adequate under a given set of facts and circumstances. The plan fiduciary is responsible for making the determination whether adequate steps were taken.

Decline in Use of Federal Government Locator Services

Notably, government locator services no longer appear to be a cost-effective method for locating Lost Participants. Previously, after e-mail and the U.S. mail proved ineffective, a popular alternative was to use the IRS Locator Service, which was a method specifically approved by the DOL in its Lost Participant guidance. However, in August 2012, the IRS eliminated that program. The IRS based its decision on the fact that "several alternative missing person locator resources, including the Internet, have become available" since 1994, when the locator service was first made available for use in locating Lost Participants. The IRS also noted that the SSA continues to maintain its program that Plan Representatives can use for locating Lost Participants. However, multiple witnesses testified that the SSA's program, which currently charges a $35 per participant fee and takes several months, is not a viable alternative for locating most Lost Participants because it is prohibitively expensive for most searches.

Changes in Technology

The Council also heard testimony that today's technology has resulted in other search methods becoming more effective. This includes web search tools, commercial locator services and credit reporting companies. Mr. Spencer and Ms. Steigerwalt testified that the use of commonly available Internet search engines (e.g., Google, Bing, Yahoo!, etc.) provide information that allowed them to locate the missing or lost participant. Mr. Williams testified that Retirement Clearinghouse had great success in using IMDB.com, a database that includes information regarding actors and similar professionals, in locating Lost Participants in a plan covering people in the entertainment business.

Mr. McHugh testified that the use of USA People Search or People Finders has proved to be successful. These Internet services are far less expensive than the SSA program, as the fee charged is usually a flat fee based on the number of participants being searched rather than on a per participant basis.

Special Circumstances

Several of the witnesses noted that certain plan-related events often triggered an effort to search for Lost Participants. Those events included plan terminations, implementation of de-risking strategies, and changes in record keepers. Under these circumstances, Plan fiduciaries were more inclined to undertake Lost Participant searches that were more extensive and costly.

Payment for Locating Lost Participants

Interestingly, most of the witnesses testified that the plan sponsor was paying for Lost Participant searches. This is the case even though ERISA permits the use of plan assets to pay for searches under certain circumstances. Several witnesses testified that they believed that passing on the costs to the plan (and thus the participants) was not appropriate because the cost was too high. Mr. Martorano noted that he saw more willingness to allow for payment from plan assets in the case of a defined contribution plan. Ms. Steigerwalt stated that she typically saw payments from defined contribution plan assets only if there was money in the forfeiture account or if the plan was terminated.

3. Strategies used in the United Kingdom and Australia

The Council also invited John Turner, Director of the Pension Policy Center, to discuss how other countries address Lost Participant issues. Mr. Turner has studied how many other western countries deal with the inter-related issues of Lost Participants (i.e., the plan cannot find the participant or beneficiary) and "lost pensions" (i.e., the participant cannot find the plan). His testimony focused on the United Kingdom and Australian pension systems as, in his view, their programs fit into a voluntary employer-sponsored benefit plan regime like the one we have in the U.S.

The United Kingdom has a single pension registry. Plan administrators are responsible for registering and notifying the registry of changes of pension plan status such as a plan termination, and changes in names and addresses. The registry provides a single source of information for participants who are trying to find their pension. Participants make an inquiry to the registry by submitting the name and last known address of their former employer. The pension registry then responds to the participant and provides contact information for the plans. The government is not involved after supplying this information to the participant. It is up to the individual to follow up and contact the pension plan after receiving information from the pension registry.

Australia, on the other hand, has approached the problem from a different perspective by establishing a lost members' register. In the event that a written communication to a participant in a pension plan comes back as undeliverable or the plan otherwise has lost contact with the employee, the pension plan is required to report detailed information on employees with whom the plan has lost contact. A participant can contact the registry either by the web or in person, and the participant is given the pension plan contact information from the registry. If the pension plan has two pieces of mail returned, the plan must register the participant as lost with the pension registry. If a participant has been lost for more than twelve months and the amount of the benefit is valued at $2,000 Australian dollars or less (to be increased to $6,000 Australian dollars by December 31, 2016), the pension account is transferred to the pension registry, where an account is maintained for the participant and interest is credited at the rate of inflation. When individuals leave Australia, they are given a form notice explaining how to claim a pension. As a result of recent government efforts, it is estimated that the number of lost pensions was reduced by 30%.

Interestingly, while the UK and Australia have different systems in that one is focused on the registration of plans while the other is focused on the registration of participants, both systems have a common component. Both countries use technology to create a centralized database designed to help assure participants and beneficiaries are connected with their plan benefits. Mr. Turner also testified that technology is the key to solving the Lost Participant/lost plan problem.

Council Observations

The workforce today has become more transient. Former employees often leave a balance in a retirement plan that goes unclaimed because the employee has forgotten about it, passed away, or because the employer no longer has a current address on file. Additionally, employer actions with regard to the plans such as terminations, mergers and spin-offs and business transactions involving the employer such as mergers, sales, divestitures, or bankruptcies can contribute to participants becoming lost or missing. Such changes to the plan or plan sponsor (e.g., changes to the plan sponsor's name or address) appear to increase Lost Participant issues. However, there are a number of steps that can be taken to minimize the number of Lost Participants and to locate those participants who do become lost.

In listening to witness testimony, reviewing statements submitted by witnesses, and considering its own research and experience, the Council gathered a considerable amount of information regarding approaches to address Lost Participant issues. The Council has several observations based upon such information.

- There are a number of different approaches to addressing Lost Participant issues. Factors considered in what approaches may or may not be taken include (i) the cost of locating the Lost Participant, (ii) the number of participants involved, (iii) the amount of the benefits involved, and (iv) whether the participant or beneficiary is required to take a distribution from the plan.
- Most Plan Representatives initially use the least expensive techniques such as first-class mail and electronic notification via e-mail, in order to comply with their fiduciary responsibilities. Some fiduciaries at that point might follow up with certified-return receipt mail and, if that is unsuccessful, determine if a more intensive search is required. The level of search will depend on the facts and circumstances.
- The SSA locator service is prohibitively expensive and not widely used by plan sponsors or service providers. Now that the IRS Letter Forwarding Service cannot be used to locate Lost Participants, plan sponsors and service providers do not have a low-cost alternative available through the federal government to resolve Lost Participant issues. Further, DOL guidance on locating Lost Participants appears to suggest that if a government locator service was used, the plan fiduciary met its obligations under ERISA. Any sense of security achieved by using a government locator service is now gone, as the only alternative is prohibitively expensive.
- Advances in information technology make available a considerable range of options to plan sponsors and service providers to locate Lost Participants. The best example of this is the use of popular search engines available on the Internet at little or no cost. Private locator sources, many of which use a combination of sources to locate Lost Participants, may be used when other methods fail. We believe it is important to emphasize that the use of this type of technology is now in the mainstream of our society and has proven reliable and effective. The DOL should seriously consider promoting the value of this technology as the primary method for locating Lost Participants.

- Plan representatives may employ processes and procedures to help reduce the number of Lost Participants. These procedures emphasize regular contact with participants throughout the entire period of plan participation (not just when the participant is an employee) and maintenance of appropriate records throughout this period.
- Many times, the first indication that a participant is lost or missing is when benefit statements or other required communications are mailed to the participant and are returned as undeliverable with no forwarding address. Also, benefit payment checks for mandatory cash outs or mandatory required distributions are returned or are not cashed. It should be noted that often mail is not returned because the current resident throws away the mail. By contrast, email that is undeliverable generally provides the sender with a bounced email notification.

Based upon the testimony, the Council made a recommendation in Section II of this report that the DOL provide information to Plan Representatives, participants and beneficiaries regarding "best practices" on how to minimize Lost Participant issues and to resolve those issues once they occur.

B. Legal Guidance on Fiduciary and Other Issues

At the suggestion of Joe Canary, Director, Office of Regulations and Interpretations, Employee Benefit Security Administration, U.S. Department of Labor, the Council reviewed a number of sources of DOL guidance that address Lost Participants.

Further, the Council reviewed several provisions of the Internal Revenue Code ("Code") and related guidance because the DOL sources addressing rollovers of Lost Participants' benefits were closely tied to these Code provisions. The Council summarizes the relevant DOL and tax-related provisions below for the purpose of determining whether those sources adequately address all Lost Participant issues.

1. U.S. Department of Labor – Locating Lost Participants & Distributions

Field Assistance Bulletin 2004-2

Field Assistance Bulletin 2004-2 (the "FAB") addresses the fiduciary responsibilities for (1) locating missing participants of a terminated defined contribution plan; and (2) distributing an account balance when efforts to communicate with a missing participant fail to secure a distribution election. In the FAB, the DOL states that a plan fiduciary has the responsibility to try and locate a missing participant before distributing the benefit from the terminating plan. Notably, because the FAB addresses terminating plans, there is some focus on getting the benefits out of the plan in order to be able to wind down the plan and trust.

The FAB provides for a number of search alternatives, one or more of which may be employed by the plan fiduciary to locate missing participants and beneficiaries. The fiduciary, in complying with ERISA's fiduciary duty provisions, should determine which of the following steps should be taken and if more than one should be taken.

- Use certified mail – return receipt requested.
- Check records of other plans offered by the sponsor.
- Check with the participant's designated beneficiary.
- Use either the Internal Revenue ("IRS") or Social Security Administration ("SSA") Letter-Forwarding Service.

The FAB states that a plan fiduciary may determine that it would be prudent to use other search options "in addition to" those listed above. Such other search options include "Internet search tools, commercial locator services, and credit reporting agencies to locate a missing participant." In the FAB, the DOL notes that if the cost of using these services will be charged to a participant's account, the fiduciary should "consider the size of the participant's account balance in relation to the cost of the services when deciding whether the use of such services is appropriate." Notably, the FAB does not make this point with regard to the governmental letter forwarding programs.

The FAB also states that if the plan fiduciary is unable "to locate participants or otherwise obtain directions concerning the distribution of their benefits," there are a number of options that the fiduciary might have with regard to effecting the distribution and thus allowing for the winding up of the terminated plan and trust. The FAB directs the plan fiduciary to consider the following options in the order described below:

- *Individual Retirement Plan Rollovers:* The DOL states that the plan fiduciary "must always consider distributing missing participant benefits into individual retirement plans (i.e., an individual retirement account or annuity)." This is the "preferred distribution option because it is more likely to preserve assets for retirement purposes than any of the other identified options." The FAB points to DOL's safe harbor regulation for selecting the individual retirement plan custodians and trustees and the investment option when the vested account balance is $5,000 or less and the plan provides for a "cash out" distribution. The DOL notes that this regulation, which can be found at 29 C.F.R. § 2550.404a-2, could be applied in the context of a DC plan termination even if the account balance was larger than $5,000.
- *Federally Insured Bank Accounts*: If the fiduciary is unable to find an individual retirement plan trustee or custodian to take the rollover, transferring the account balance to an interest bearing federally insured bank account in the name of a missing participant is permissible if the participant would have an unconditional right to withdraw funds from the account. The fiduciary should consider the interest rate paid on the account and bank charges in determining whether such a transfer is prudent and otherwise in compliance with ERISA.
- *Escheat to State Unclaimed Property Funds*: As an alternative, plan fiduciaries may also consider transferring missing participants' account balances to state unclaimed property funds in the state of each participant's last known residence or work location. The FAB states that this option is a possibility if the individual retirement solution will not work. However, the FAB does not appear to require the fiduciary to attempt a transfer to a federally insured bank account prior to escheating.

In the FAB, the DOL rejected the resolution of causing a distribution by withholding for federal income tax purposes the entire distribution and sending it to the Treasury.

The Council notes that the FAB only applies to terminated defined contribution plans. The specific application of the FAB to terminating plans raises the question whether, in the view of the DOL, all of the guidance in the FAB (including distribution options after unsuccessful attempts to locate the participant or beneficiary) can be the basis for addressing Lost Participants in a non-terminated plan. The Council heard testimony that plan fiduciaries typically look at the FAB for guidance on addressing such issues for non-terminated plans. However, at least one witness requested that the FAB be extended to non-terminated plans as well. Also, the Council received testimony that it is not clear (i) whether all of the guidance in the FAB can be applied to lost beneficiaries and (ii)what part of the guidance applies to non-terminated plans.

Automatic Rollover Safe Harbor Regulations – Final Rule

In September of 2004, the DOL issued final regulations, 29 C.F.R. § 2550.404a–2, regarding the automatic rollover of cash out distributions from a defined contribution plan to an individual retirement plan. The DOL issued that regulation in response to a change in the tax code applicable to mandatory cash distributions ranging from $1,000 to $5,000. If a plan provides for a mandatory cash out, the Code requires the plan to send a notice to the participant stating that the participant is required to receive a distribution and, if the participant does not respond to the notice, the cash out distribution will be automatically rolled over to an IRA.

That regulation sets forth certain requirements related to notice and investment of IRA assets that, if met, would create a safe harbor under ERISA's fiduciary provisions in connection with the rollover distribution. In the preamble to the regulation, the DOL noted that some commenters to the proposed safe harbor rule suggested that the safe harbor be extended to distributions of benefits to missing participants in a terminated defined contribution plan. However, the DOL did not extend the safe harbor to missing participants because "these issues are beyond the scope of this safe harbor initiative on mandatory rollover distributions." Furthermore, the regulation, at least on its face, does not address beneficiaries.

The Council received testimony from Mr. McHugh that the DOL regulation has shortcomings. The regulation appears to address only mandatory distributions prescribed by the Code to plan participants. However, from a plan administrator's standpoint, the real challenge is addressing mandatory distributions pursuant to the terms of the plan to beneficiaries. Many plans immediately require distributions to beneficiaries upon the death of the participant. Unlike mandatory cash outs to participants, the amount of the distribution may substantially exceed $5,000. However, the DOL regulation does not appear to provide safe harbor protection to a plan fiduciary that caused such a distribution to be rolled over to an IRA. In fact, the preamble states that the DOL regulation is not intended to address Lost

Participant issues. Furthermore, as discussed below, the DOL's regulations that address rollovers in a Lost Participant situation only apply in the context of a plan termination.

Termination of Abandoned Individual Account Plans - Final Rule

In April of 2006, the DOL issued regulations, 29 C.F.R. § 2578.1 and 29 C.F.R. § 2550.404(a)-3, and a related prohibited transaction class exemption, specifically addressing the distribution of benefits from a terminated defined contribution plan when a participant or beneficiary was missing or nonresponsive. More specifically, the DOL issued final regulations addressing the distribution of participant account balances from (i) a defined contribution plan that was abandoned by the plan sponsor (and terminated as part of the DOL's abandoned plan procedures) and (ii) any defined contributions plan that was terminated. The DOL noted in the preamble to those regulations that the final safe harbor regulation related to distributions from any terminated defined contributions plan "codifies those parts of Field Assistance Bulletin 2004–02 (September 30, 2004) relating to the distribution of assets to an individual retirement plan from terminating individual account plans in those instances where a participant or beneficiary fails to make a distribution election."

The regulations create a safe harbor under ERISA's fiduciary duty provisions. In both regulations, the DOL provides that in the event notices informing plan participants or beneficiaries about the plan termination and their plan benefits were returned as undeliverable, the plan fiduciary is required to "take steps to locate and provide notice to the participant or beneficiary" before making a distribution from the plan. Such "steps" would include those in FAB 2004-02. However, if after taking such steps the plan fiduciary cannot locate the participant or beneficiary, the plan may distribute the participant or beneficiary's account balance (regardless of the size of the account balance).

In the case of any terminated defined contribution plan, a distribution to a missing or nonresponsive participant or spousal beneficiary could be made to an individual retirement plan established on behalf of the missing or nonresponsive participant/beneficiary if certain requirements were met. In the case of a non-spouse beneficiary, the law at that time did not allow for rollovers by such beneficiaries. Thus, the distribution amount could be transferred to an account (other than an individual retirement plan) maintained by a financial institution that can offer individual retirement accounts (e.g., most banks). The DOL concluded that in the case of any terminated defined contribution plan, whether terminated in the normal course or through the abandoned plan program, the rollover could be completed under the safe harbor even if the amount of the account balance exceeded $5,000. In 2007, the DOL updated this regulation to reflect a change in the Code allowing for rollover distributions to "inherited IRAs."

In addition, the DOL added a *de minimis* exception for account balances under $1,000. In the case of an abandoned plan that was terminated as a part of the DOL's abandoned plan program, the regulations provide for a *de minimis* exception whereby the financial services company would not be required to cause a rollover distribution to an IRA. Rather, such amounts could be transferred to an interest-bearing bank account or state unclaimed property fund. The DOL added this exception in response to comments to the proposed regulation that financial institutions would not want to utilize the abandoned plan program if it was required to take such rollovers into its own IRA product or find another provider that would take them.

This regulation only applies to terminated defined contributions plans. Therefore, the safe harbor is not available in the event the plan is not terminated, but a distribution event has otherwise occurred; even if the distribution is otherwise mandated by the terms of the plan and/or the Code.

2. Internal Revenue Service

As noted above, the DOL regulations related to Lost Participant rollover distributions are closely tied to Code provisions that allow or require such rollover distributions. The Code imposes limits on the ability of a plan to immediately distribute a participant's benefit. These limits impact what steps a plan can take to pay out benefits attributable to Lost Participants. Furthermore, the Code mandates when a plan must begin making distributions. It is unclear how this requirement can be met for benefits payable to Lost Participants.

Sections 411(a)(11) and 401(a)(31) of the Code generally provide that a plan cannot distribute a participant's benefit upon his or her termination from employment before normal retirement age if the vested benefit is greater than $5,000. However, if the participant's vested accrued benefit is less than $5,000, the plan may provide for the employment. These are often called "cash out distributions" or simply "cash outs." However, if the plan provides for such cash outs and the vested accrued benefit is at least $1,000, the plan must notify the participant about the pending cash out and, if the participant is non-responsive, the plan administrator is required to rollover the cash out distribution to an individual retirement plan. It was this rollover requirement that led to the DOL's safe harbor regulations discussed above under

"Automatic Rollover Safe Harbor Regulations – Final Rule." For vested accrued benefits of less than $1,000, the plan can simply pay out the distribution to the participant without providing the rollover option. Notably, the $5,000 limit and the automatic rollover provisions do not apply to beneficiaries.

Notwithstanding the general prohibition against "cash out" distributions of participant benefits in excess of $5,000, a plan may provide that a participant is required to receive a distribution after termination from employment upon reaching the later of age sixty-two or normal retirement age as defined by the plan. Further, Section 401(a)(9) of the Code requires that a plan begin making required minimum distributions from the plan after the participant terminates employment in the year following the year in which the participant attains age 70-1/2. There are also minimum required distribution rules applicable to spouse and non spouse beneficiaries.

3. Interconnection between DOL and IRS Guidance

The DOL guidance on dealing with Lost Participants and the IRS guidance related to plan distributions are very much inter-connected. If a plan provides for cash outs of under $1,000, the plan's service provider will cause a distribution and generate a check for a relatively small amount of money. At that point, the plan administrator may become aware of a bad address because the check, sent via regular mail, is returned to the trustee as undeliverable. This clearly raises a Lost Participant issue and indicates the plan fiduciary should begin some kind of search process. However, in some cases those checks are not returned and simply go uncashed. At this point, the plan has no idea whether the lack of response indicates the participant received the check and simply did not cash it or whether the participant never received the check. A question then arises as to what may be done with the funds underlying that uncashed distribution check. These funds are typically held in a bank checking or other depository account. In addition, these accounts may be specific to the plan and treated as part of the trust assets or may be held outside the trust, which is typically the case when omnibus accounts are used.

When a check remains uncashed, the plan fiduciary must decide what to do with the funds underlying the uncashed check. Since the participant is subject to the cash out rule, re-establishing the participant's account within the plan allows the participant to effectively negate the cash out provision simply by failing to negotiate the check. Therefore, a common practice is to transfer those amounts to the plan's forfeiture account after the plan fiduciary has taken reasonable steps to attempt to locate and notify the participant or beneficiary. At that point, the distribution amount returned to the plan is treated just like any other forfeiture under the plan's terms. If the participant later requests his or her benefit amount, the plan will pay the benefit without adjustments for investment gains or losses that might have been earned from the date of forfeiture to the participant. A description of this procedure should be included in the plan document and summary plan description. The Treasury regulations, 26 C.F.R. § 1.411(a)-11, support forfeiture under these circumstances.

If the plan provides for cash outs of amounts in excess of $1,000 and up to $5,000, a notice must be sent to the participant asking whether the participant would prefer an immediate cash distribution or a rollover to an IRA. If the participant does not respond, the plan administrator is required to rollover the account to an IRA. However, in the event the notice is returned as undeliverable, the plan administrator may not be able to effect the rollover to an IRA and still rely on the DOL safe harbor discussed above under "Automatic Rollover Safe Harbor Regulations – Final Rule." As discussed above, the DOL specifically did not address the use of the safe harbor in the context of Lost Participants. Since that time, the DOL's regulations only focus on distributions to Lost Participants in the event of a plan termination.

Similar issues arise when a distribution is required to be made from the plan either because the plan requires a distribution at age 62 or normal retirement age, or the plan requires a distribution by reason of the required minimum distribution requirements at age 70-1/2. At that point, certain distribution notices, such as a tax notice required under Section 402(f) of the Code, may be returned as undeliverable, preventing the distribution from being made. Thus, the distribution cannot be made. If the plan is unable to make distributions mandated by the Code and the terms of the plan, the plan runs the risk of jeopardizing its tax-qualified status because the plan is not being administered pursuant to its terms, which is defined as an "operational failure" by the IRS. The Council heard testimony from the PSCA and American Benefits Council that plan fiduciaries are put in a difficult situation when they face the required distribution for Code purposes; but the DOL has not issued direct guidance on the fiduciaries' responsibilities in these circumstances.

Furthermore, if the distribution is made and the distribution check goes uncashed, a question arises as to what should happen to the distribution amount. While returning the distribution amount to the plan as described above for cash outs might be an option, this seems less palatable when the plan and the Code require the distribution. Rollover to an IRA might be an option (to the extent the rollover is otherwise permitted under the Code). Unfortunately, as noted above, the DOL's safe harbor rollover guidance only applies to terminated plans.

4. DOL Guidance on Preemption, State Abandoned Property Laws, and Lost Participants

Every state has enacted laws that require the holder of property that has been abandoned to transfer such property to the state. On several occasions, and as noted by Mr. Canary in his testimony, DOL has issued guidance indicating its view that ERISA Section 514(a) preempts application of these state abandoned property laws to plan benefits. The earliest guidance is in Advisory Opinion 78-32A, where DOL stated that ERISA preempts an Illinois abandoned property law specifically applicable to property held in a fiduciary capacity. In Advisory Opinion 79-31, DOL similarly stated that ERISA preempts a California law providing that employee benefit trust distributions escheat to the state if the owner has not indicated an interest in the benefit within seven years after the distribution becomes payable. The DOL most recently expressed its view in Advisory Opinion 94-41A, where DOL concluded that ERISA preempts application of a Texas unclaimed property law to a defined contribution plan. The DOL stated:

> It is the view of the Department of Labor (the Department) that, if the above-quoted section of the Texas Unclaimed Property Statutes were applied to require the Plan to pay to the State amounts held in the Terminated Employees' Account, or in other accounts of the Plan, pursuant to the procedures described above, then such application of the section would be preempted under section 514(a) of ERISA. Such an application of the State escheat law would directly affect the core functions of the Plan by reducing, through the escheat, the amount of plan assets held in trust for the benefit of all participants and beneficiaries of the Plan. Moreover, because the statute at issue is not a law regulating insurance, banking or securities, it is not saved from preemption under section 514(b)(2).

Numerous witnesses indicated that plans uniformly treat benefits of Lost Participants as not subject to state abandoned property laws. This preemption of state law allows plans to follow uniform procedures with respect to benefits of Lost Participants regardless of the state of residence. It appears that state abandoned property administrators respect ERISA preemption and do not attempt to subject benefits of participants in ongoing plans to escheatment.

Some witnesses suggested that DOL could provide guidance that would permit plans to turn over property on a voluntary basis to state abandoned property authorities as a method of handling the accounts of missing participants. Most members of the Council do not support this approach because the resulting patchwork of state and federal regulation would introduce further complexity that is unlikely to result in uniting participants with their benefits.

The Council also noted that there is no guidance on ERISA preemption in the context of benefits of missing participants in terminated plans. If the PBGC implements its missing participant program for terminated DC plans, the issue of ERISA preemption may become moot. However, in the absence of such a program, the question of application of ERISA preemption to benefits in terminated DC plans remains unresolved.

5. DOL Guidance - Plan Asset and Accounting Treatment of Uncashed Benefit Checks

Many DC plan record keepers use omnibus accounts to process distributions to participants. When a participant takes a distribution, the participant's account in the plan is liquidated and the funds are transferred to an omnibus account that is used to effect payment to the participant. Typically, assets remain in the omnibus account only for the period of time it takes the participant to negotiate payment of the check – usually a matter of just a few days. However, if a participant is lost, unresponsive or otherwise does not negotiate the check, the assets remain in the account until steps are taken to return the funds to the plan. Although the DOL provided guidance, FAB 2002-3, on the handling of float associated with omnibus accounts, there is currently no legal guidance on the status of these assets while they remain in the omnibus account.

Typically, checks that go uncashed represent distributions of small account balances or residual amounts allocated to participants after they have already taken the bulk of their account in an earlier distribution. As discussed above, cash out distributions of $1,000 or more that have not been requested by the participant are automatically rolled over to an IRA. All other distributions before retirement age are distributed only with participant consent so are unlikely to remain uncashed. However, in the case of distributions after retirement age, including minimum required distributions after age 70-1/2, it is possible that checks for significantly larger amounts will remain uncashed. In any case, uncashed checks can accumulate over time and represent a significant amount for larger plans.

The lack of certainty over the status of assets associated with these uncashed checks has been of increasing concern to the accounting industry. DOL regulations require the auditor to form an opinion on whether the plan's financial statements are presented fairly, in all material respects, in accordance with the applicable reporting framework.

However, if the status of assets in omnibus accounts is unclear, plan management does not know how or when to report the assets on the plan's financial statements. James Haubrock, testifying on behalf of the American Institute of Certified Public Accountants, indicated that practice varies in this area and recommended that DOL issue guidance on both the plan assets status of uncashed checks and reporting on IRS Form 5500.

Council Observations

The Council believes that while FAB 2004-2 and the other guidance issued by the DOL in relation to Lost Participants issues serves as a useful guide for plan fiduciaries, the DOL could unify and clarify that guidance in order to make it more helpful to plan fiduciaries in resolving Lost Participant issues. The Council identified several areas where the DOL guidance could use updating, consolidation, or clarification:

- FAB 2004-2 (i) does not address certain Internet search tools that have become part of the mainstream such as search engines available through Internet service providers and (ii) does not specifically address whether the guidance applies to beneficiaries. Further, the focus on the governmental letter forwarding programs is out of date with the elimination of the IRS program, leaving only the SSA program, which is prohibitively expensive.
- FAB 2004-2 does not address searches for and distributions to Lost Participants related to non-terminated plans. Many plan fiduciaries apply the principles in the FAB in attempting to locate Lost Participants in non-terminated plans. However, the applicability of the guidance in the FAB on handling distributions to Lost Participants is not readily apparent in a non-terminated plan. In the latter situation, not all participants and beneficiaries are entitled to a distribution and the plan fiduciaries are not attempting to remove all assets from the plan as part of the plan wind down process.

- Plans may be in a position where there are a number of beneficiaries required to receive an immediate cash out distribution from the plan. However, if the beneficiaries cannot be located or are unresponsive, the current DOL safe harbor regulations addressing rollovers of mandatory cash out distributions to IRAs do not apply in the event the plan administrator wishes to cause a rollover to an IRA on behalf of such beneficiaries.
- Plans may be in a position where the plan terms and the Code require a distribution to a participant (e.g., upon reaching normal retirement age or age 70-1/2). However, the DOL does not have regulations that address whether such distributions may be rolled over to an IRA (to the extent otherwise permitted under the Code). The DOL regulation that provides for a safe harbor only applies to defined contribution plans that are terminated. Therefore, plan fiduciaries are put in the difficult position of making distributions to meet the Code requirements, but no clear path on how to do so and meet the ERISA fiduciary requirements.
- The existing guidance on ERISA preemption of state abandoned property laws is dated and does not address preemption in all contexts, including application of the rules with respect to benefits associated with terminated plans.
- The lack of guidance on the plan asset status of funds held in omnibus accounts has resulted in varied accounting practices and inconsistent reporting on Form 5500.

Based upon our analysis, observations, and witness testimony, the Council made several recommendations in Section II of this paper regarding how the DOL can improve its regulatory and sub-regulatory guidance that touches on Lost Participant issues.

C. Developing an Integrated Regulatory Regime

The Council looked at other programs and agencies of the federal government to identify whether those agencies and the DOL could better coordinate their activities in order to resolve Lost Participant issues. The Council surmised that certain mechanisms may already exist within the current retirement system that could be used to resolve Lost Participant as well as lost pension issues. Additionally, the Council heard testimony regarding a number of legal requirements and programs that may be helpful in resolving Lost Participant issues or minimizing the occurrence of Lost Participants. These issues include reporting of terminated vested participants under Code Section 6057, the PBGC's lost participant pension registry and government-funded pension counseling programs.

1. Code Section 6057 Reporting of Pension Benefits of Terminated VestedParticipants to Internal Revenue Service and Disclosure through Social Security Administration

Code Section 6057(a) requires the administrator of a pension plan subject to ERISA's vesting provisions to file a registration statement with the Secretary of Treasury. The registration statement sets forth: (i) certain information related to the plan, (ii) plan participants who separate from serviced covered by the plan and are entitled to deferred vested retirement benefits, and (iii) the nature, amount and forms of deferred vested retirement benefits in which the plan participants are entitled. Code Section 6057(b) provides that any plan administrator required to register under Section 6057(a) shall, within the time prescribed by regulation, also notify the Secretary of Treasury of any change in the name of the plan or the names and address of the plan administrator, the termination of the plan, or the merger or consolidation of the plan with any other plan or its division into two or more plans.

Until January 1, 2009, pension plan administrators complied with reporting obligations under Code Section 6057(a) by filing Schedule SSA to the Form 5500. The reporting requirements of 6057(b) are met by completing certain questions on Form 5500. On the form, the plan administrator was required to identify the plan sponsor (Question 2a), the plan sponsor's employer identification number (Question 2b), the plan administrator (Question 3a), and the plan administrator's employer identification number (Question 3b). Furthermore, if the name and/or the employer identification number of the plan sponsor had changed since the last Form 5500 filing, the plan administrator was required to report the plan sponsor name, employer identification number, and the plan number from the last From 5500 filing.

Starting January 1, 2009, the DOL's final regulation requires the filing of electronic Form 5500s and the Schedule SSA was eliminated. On March 3, 2011, the IRS issued Announcement 2011-21, which provided that for purposes of Code Section 6057(a) reporting [initial disclosure of terminated vested participants], pension plan administrators would use new IRS Form

8955-SSA to replace Form 5500 Schedule SSA. For purposes of Code Section 6057(b) [disclosures of changes of address, and identity of the pension plan], plan administrators were instructed to continue using Form 5500.

Code Section 6057(d) requires the Secretary of Treasury to transmit copies of any statements, notifications, reports or other information obtained by the Secretary under Section 6057, to the SSA. The SSA is required to notify a participant that he or she may be eligible to receive a pension benefit on a form letter titled "Potential Private Retirement Benefit Information." The notification is generally triggered by the participant's becoming eligible for social security benefits. This form letter directs the participant to the toll-free phone number of EBSA and its address in Washington, as well as a toll-free phone number of the SSA if the participant has a problem locating the pension plan.

Based upon the Council's review of this regulatory regime, the Council believes that the current system of reporting information on terminated vested participants is not optimal. First, the system does not adequately keep a record of a legacy plan which has been the subject to changes, such as a plan merger into a consolidated plan. A participant in a legacy plan which has been merged likely may not be notified by the SSA that the plan has been merged and about post-plan merger changes in the address or plan administrator. Second, a terminated vested participant may be reported by the plan administrator on the Form 8955-SSA and receive a distribution shortly thereafter. Years later when the former participant applies for Social Security benefits, he will receive the form letter stating that he "may" have a pension. Unnecessary confusion for participants and administrative expense for plans could be avoided if the Code Section 6057 information is updated for plan distributions. A correction of both of these problems would likely require modifications in Form 5500 and Form 8955-SSA.

2. PBGC Lost Participant Pension Registry

For years, the PBGC has provided a lost participant program for participants and beneficiaries in terminated, single employer defined benefit pension plans, as required by ERISA Section 4050. That program is not applicable to defined contribution plans. However, the Pension Protection Act of 2006 provides for the PBGC's implementation of a program to accommodate terminated defined contributions plans and multiemployer plans. To date, the PBGC has not implemented this program. On June 21, 2013, the PBGC issued an RFI in which it solicited comments from the public regarding interest in a terminated defined contribution plan program and other information.

Under the existing PBGC program, if the plan has a "missing participant," such a plan is required to transfer the benefit to the PBGC. Furthermore, the PBGC maintains a website which can be searched by a person who believes he or she may be entitled to a pension benefit that has been transmitted to the PBGC under its missing participant program. In addition, the website refers the public to the PBGC publication "Finding a Lost Pension," which was a joint project of the PBGC and the Pension Action Center. This publication is written in layperson's language on how to find a lost pension. The publication includes a list of EBSA offices and pension counseling programs funded by the Division of Aging of the United States Department of Health and Human Services.

Ms. Deborah Murphy, Senior Counsel in the Office of the General Counsel of the PBGC, testified that the PBGC was reviewing the comments it received through the aforementioned RFI. She noted that there was public interest in a missing participant program for terminated defined contribution plans as well as for active defined contribution plans. The commenters stated that, in developing such a program, the PBGC should coordinate its activities with the DOL and the SEC as they both have rules related to Lost Participants. Ms. Murphy drafted the current PBGC regulation on lost participants for terminated single employer defined pension plans and indicated that she will be involved with the drafting of any regulations implementing the expansion of the PBGC pension registry for terminated defined contribution plans which was provided for by the Pension Protection Act. Ms. Murphy testified that some plan administrators do not perform an adequate search before a benefit of a lost participant is turned over to the PBGC under its current program and that she believes the current PBGC standard is higher than that required under applicable law. Accordingly, the PBGC likely will require a high level of searching for a lost participant before a benefit or account is turned over to the PBGC.

In general, the Council is supportive of a PBGC sponsored program made available to terminated defined contribution plans as set forth in the Pension Protection Act. Such a program would be helpful in alleviating some of the administrative burdens associated with resolving Lost Participant issues. However, close coordination between the DOL and the PBGC is necessary to make this program useful.

3. Pension Counseling Programs Funded by HHS under the Older Americans Act of 1965

Section 215 of the Older Americans Act of 1965, as amended, provides that the Administration on Aging of the United States Department of Health and Human Services is authorized to award grants to eligible entities "to establish and carry out pension counseling and information programs that create or continue a sufficient number of pension assistance and counseling programs to provide outreach, information, counseling, referral, and other assistance regarding pension and other retirement benefits. . . ." The Pension Action Center in Boston Massachusetts is one of six funded pension counseling programs. Currently, 29 states have a pension counseling project funded by Section 215 of the Older Americans Act. The Pension Action Center partnered with the PBGC in drafting the publication "Finding a Lost Pension" discussed above.

Ms. Ellen Bruce, Director of the Pension Action Center, testified that in 2004 she and John Turner published a paper which estimated that lost pension participants in the United States had over $100 billion in unclaimed benefits. Ms. Bruce testified that a participant may become lost to a pension plan as a result of corporate mergers, bankruptcy and shut downs which can occur in the intervening years between employment termination and an application for retirement benefits. Similarly, Ms. Jane Smith, Policy Analyst for the Pension Rights Center, testified that a participant may become lost due to changes in an employer's name, merger, spin-off or shut down. Ms. Bruce testified that a lost participant inquiry is frequently initiated when a participant receives a "you may have a pension" letter from SSA.

Ms. Bruce encouraged the enhancement of the PBGC's current missing participants and related registry as indicated in the Pension Protection Act of 2006. Ms. Bruce also recommended expanding the pension counseling programs under Section 215 of the Older Americans Act to include all fifty states. She testified that such programs have a record of success. Ms. Smith further explained that the Pension Rights Center supports an amendment to ERISA Section 4051 introduced by Congressman Neal (H.R. 2127), which would provide for a lost plan pension registry. On the registry, a plan sponsor would record the history of plans (including plan mergers, changes in sponsor, etc.). The PSCA also testified that it supported this amendment. Mr. McHugh noted that the registry could make the SSA's notification process stemming from the Form 8955-SSA more useful, as the recipients of that notice could then go to the registry. In the event that this amendment was enacted, Ms.

Smith recommended that the DOL should revisit existing regulatory guidance on due diligence searches for lost participants to include use of the expanded PBGC registry.

Council Observations

Based upon its own research and witness testimony, the Council identified several areas under current law that may provide significant safeguards to address Lost Participant issues. Many of those safeguards involve agencies other than the DOL and included the IRS, PBGC and the SSA. Further, the Council learned that the issues of Lost Participants and "lost pensions" are closely related. With regard to the Lost Participants, the plan sponsor still exists and is well aware that it has one or more participants entitled to a benefit who cannot be located or who are not responsive. In the "lost pension" scenario, the participant believes that he or she is entitled to a pension, but cannot locate the employer for any number of reasons. Presumably, by taking actions to reduce the number of "lost pensions," some Lost Participant issues can be resolved and vice versa.

The Council also made several other observations:

- Code Section 6057(a), (b), and (c) do not appear to be effective in assuring that plans and plan participants stay connected, particularly over long periods of time.
- There does not appear to be a great deal of coordination among the DOL, IRS, SSA and PBGC in addressing Lost Participant and "lost pension" issues.
- Additional efforts could be made to expand the availability of pension counseling programs and making participants and beneficiaries aware of these programs.
- The DOL should work closely with the PBGC in the PBGC's development of a defined contribution missing participant program or similar programs to assure that each agency is establishing consistent standards for locating Lost Participants.

Based upon our analysis, observations, and witness testimony, the Council made several recommendations in Section II of this paper regarding how the DOL, Treasury, IRS, and SSA can better coordinate their activities so as to help minimize the occurrence of Lost Participants (and the related occurrence of "lost pensions"), and its regulatory and sub-regulatory guidance that touches on Lost Participants issues. The Council asks that DOL share this paper with these agencies in order to promote inter-agency cooperation on these issues.

IV. Concluding Observations

After hearing witness testimony, reviewing written statements, and conducting its own research, the Council believes that there are useful steps which plans, participants and governmental agencies can take to ensure that participants remain connected with their benefits. For plans, the steps include maintaining and updating contact information and prompt searches for participants when the contact information is no longer valid. For participants, the steps include being responsible for keeping plans informed of their contact information or consolidating assets in their new employer's plan or an IRA. The government steps include DOL guidance on plan sponsor responsibilities with respect to Lost Participants and better coordination of DOL, PBGC and SSA programs designed to ensure that benefits are paid as intended. The Council recognizes that no single step will solve all Lost Participant problems. However, the Council hopes that through the combined efforts of plans, participants and governmental programs, both the administrative burden and the incidence of Lost Participants will be greatly reduced.

In: 401(k) Plans
Editor: Suzanne Abbott

ISBN: 978-1-63482-598-6

Chapter 3

TESTIMONY OF JOHN A. TURNER, DIRECTOR, PENSION POLICY CENTER. HEARING ON "LOCATING MISSING AND LOST PARTICIPANTS"*

Good morning. My name is John A. Turner. I am Director of the Pension Policy Center. I commend the ERISA Advisory Council for addressing the issue of lost pensions. This is an area where government policy can improve the retirement income security of American workers. I and my coauthors have published a number of papers on this topic, which I have included in the list of references at the end of this testimony, some of them containing a more detailed and wider ranging discussion of the issues (e.g., Blake and Turner 2001, Bruce and Turner 2004).

Although we live in the Information Age, the problems discussed here are largely problems of information management. With electronic filings of Form 5500 returns by employers and income tax forms by workers, information management should be considerably easier now than in the past.

The American workforce is mobile, many workers holding more than one job providing pensions over their careers. Many retirees face great difficulties in locating their former employers from years in the past in order to apply for a pension to which they are entitled. At the same time, pension plans have

---

* This is an edited, reformatted and augmented version of testimony presented August 28, 2013 before the Advisory Council on Employee Welfare and Pension Benefit Plans (aka ERISA Advisory Council).

trouble locating prospective pensioners who have moved and with whom they have lost contact.

The problem of lost pensions and lost pensioners was also prevalent in the United Kingdom and Australia, but these countries have established national pension registries. These registries have helped thousands of people receive their pension entitlements. I will discuss what lessons we can learn from their experience. I will then discuss how New Zealand's pension system has greatly reduced the problem of lost pensions. Lastly, I will present a proposal for sending lost defined contribution pension funds to the Social Security OASI Trust Fund so that they can be used for their designated purpose of providing retirement security.

LOST PENSIONS IN THE UNITED KINGDOM

Since 1991, the United Kingdom has had a national pension plan registry so that workers need only contact a single source to trace a lost pension (Government of the United Kingdom 2013). Workers can request assistance by telephone, mail or the Internet. The location of this registry within the government has changed with various reorganizations. Since 2005, the Pension Tracing Service has been part of the Department for Work and Pensions, under The Pensions Regulator. This Department corresponds to the Employee Benefits Security Administration under the Department of Labor.

The Pensions Regulator has responsibility for the Pension Schemes Registry, which maintains a record of the addresses and other basic details of all pension plans in operation in the UK. The term scheme is used in the UK to refer to a pension plan. Pension plan administrators are responsible for registering pension plans with The Pension Regulator and notifying that agency of changes in the status of the plan, including terminating the plan. The registration with The Pension Regulator is used for maintaining the Pension Schemes Registry. All plans registering are given a Pension Schemes Registry number, which they use in communications with The Pension Regulator.

The Pension Tracing Service in The Pensions Regulator helps workers find a pension even if the workers are not sure of the contact details. It has access to information on over 200,000 pension plans, primarily through the Pension Schemes Registry. The Pension Tracing Service uses this database, free of charge, to search for a person's pension.

Workers in the United Kingdom filing a tracing request form with the Pension Tracing Service are asked information such as the full name and last known address of the former employer. The tracing service then tries to find a current address for the pension fund.

The British government maintains the Pension Tracing Service without charging a fee to its users on the grounds that it provides an important social service. The cost of the service averages out to be about $0.20 per participant per year (Blake and Turner 2001). Using that as the basis for a cost estimate for the United States, with 130 million total participants in 2010 (US DOL 2012), the total cost would be about $26 million a year.

The tracing service does not contact pension plans on behalf of workers, but instead provides contact information. It is up to the individual to then contact their former pension plan provider. A weakness of this approach is that 28 percent of users in a recent survey did not follow up and make contact with their former employer, the most common reason stated being that they were too busy (Shury and Koerbitz 2010).

The Pension Tracing Service provides this service both for employer-provided plans and for individual account plans, which would correspond to Individual Retirement Accounts (IRAs) in the United States. More than 90 percent of the users of the service, however, use it to contact employer-provided plans (Shury and Koerbitz 2010).

Most persons using the service are near retirement age or older. A survey conducted in 2009 found that nearly half (48 percent) of the users of the Pension Tracing Service were ages 55-64, and an additional 16 percent were ages 65 and older (Shury and Koerbitz 2010). That survey found a rate in providing contact information of 75 percent. Of those provided contact information, 28 percent had not followed up as of the time of the survey and actually made the contact.

Among workers who did make contact, respondents reported in 80 percent of cases that the contact details provided by the Pension Tracing Service were correct. Of those persons with correct contact information, respondents were able to establish their eligibility to access the pension in 43 per cent of cases.

In the fiscal year 2009-2010, the Pension Tracing Service received 83,000 requests. A survey of 2,000 users of the service found that 7 percent had received lump sums of more than £20,000 (BBC 2010).

Based on all inquiries processed by the Pension Tracing Service, the outcome for around one in five of pensions (19 per cent) is that the respondent's eligibility to draw the pension had been confirmed. The low success rate may be due in part to the fact that 64 percent of the searches were for a job ending between 20 and 40 years previously. A reason for the long lag is that often people initiated searches when they were preparing to retire.

Another reason for the low success rate, which would not apply to the same extent in the United States, is the historical development of vesting requirements in the United Kingdom. There was no compulsory vesting until the early 1980s, when five-year vesting was instituted. Thus, many of the people recalling pension coverage early in their careers may not have been vested.

LOST PENSIONS IN AUSTRALIA

For more than a decade, the Australian Tax Office (ATO) has maintained a Lost Members Register. All pension funds are required to provide details of members with whom they have lost contact. Providers of individual retirement savings accounts are also required to register the names of account holders whom they are unable to contact because they no longer have a valid address for them, and who have not contributed within a specified period of time. That information is required to be provided to the government within four months of the end of each half year (www.ato.gov.au). If the pension fund has one piece of mail to a member returned unclaimed, it may report the member as lost. If it has two pieces of mail returned unclaimed, it is required to report the member as lost.

If a worker is unable to contact a former pension plan, the worker can contact the Australian Tax Office using a service called SuperSeeker (Australian Tax Office 2013). Super refers to superannuation, which is the Australian term for an employer-provided pension. Workers need to register online to use SuperSeeker. They provide identifying information, including their tax identification number (called the tax file number TFN), and date of birth.

For workers using this service, the worker's plan will presumably have contacted the Australian Tax Office because of the inability of the plan to contact the worker, so that through the Lost Members Register a connection can be made between the worker and the plan through tracking by the tax identification number.

If the government, the person's employer, or their pension fund are unable to find a participant, the participant has not made a contribution for 12 months, and the amount in the fund is A$2,000 or less, the money is transferred to the Australian Tax Office, where an account is established for that person. (Australian dollars are roughly equivalent in value to U.S. dollars.) The Government will further increase the account balance threshold to A$2,500 from 31 December 2015, and to A$3,000 from 31 December 2016. Subsequently in August 2013 the government has announced these thresholds will actually increase to A$4,000 for 31 December 2015 and A$6,000 by 31 December 2016, but these changes have not yet been enacted into law. Part of the motivation for this aspect of the program is to protect small accounts from being eroded by fees charged by financial institutions.

The government pays interest on these accounts at a rate equal to the inflation rate as measured by the Consumer Price Index, but does not charge a fee for managing the accounts. If the government subsequently is able to contact the person through their tax identification number, the person is notified of the account. In the future, probably within a year or two, if the person has changed jobs and has established a new pension account, the government notifies the person that the funds will automatically be transferred to that account unless the person requests otherwise.

The Lost Members Register database originally was searched by government employees on behalf of persons making an inquiry. Now individuals have four options. They can search online, with the possible matches reported back to them on-line. The search is based on the person's name, date of birth, and tax filing number. They can search using a self-help telephone number. They can search by calling a telephone number and speaking to a government representative. They can search by printing off information from the website and mailing in a request. Similarly to the program in the United Kingdom, it is then up to the individual to follow-up.

The Australian government also provides a tool for obtaining contact information for pension funds, called the Super Fund Lookup. That tool can be used online by keying in the name of a pension fund (Australian Government 2013b).

Many of the lost accounts without proper identification originated during the time when individuals did not have to quote a tax file number when opening an account. Now there is a substantial tax penalty if no TFN is quoted.

For a lost member's register to be successful people need to be aware of it. When a person searches for the Australian Tax Office using Google, one of the subheadings that appears under the Australian Tax Office is Super Seeker. In addition, when a person leaves Australia for a trip out of the country, he or she is given a form that includes information for finding a lost pension. If the person is not an Australian or New Zealand citizen, they may claim their account when they leave the country. If they do not make a claim, the money goes to the Australian Tax Office as unclaimed money.

The cumulative effect of various Australian government initiatives to reduce the number of lost pensions is that over the 18 months ending at the end of 2012, the number of lost pensions was reduced by 30 percent, from 5.0 million to 3.5 million (Australian Government 2013a).

New Zealand

In New Zealand, the problem of lost pensions is addressed proactively through portability of pensions. If a worker who changes jobs maintains the same pension service provider, the likelihood of a lost pension is virtually eliminated. In the defined contribution Kiwi Saver program, when a worker changes jobs, the worker takes the pension to the new job. The problem of employers having pensions from different service providers is solved by the government providing a pension clearinghouse. The employer transmits the pension contributions for the worker to the government clearinghouse, along with identifying information about the worker. The government then transmits the worker's contributions to the appropriate service provider.

A new agreement, starting July 1, 2013, allows transfer of pension balances to and from Australian superannuation funds and New Zealand Kiwisaver accounts.

A Proposal for the Ultimate Disposition of Lost Pension Funds

I conclude this testimony by drawing attention to a proposal I made a decade ago with Ellen A. Bruce for the disposition of lost pension funds in defined contribution plans and Individual Retirement Accounts (Bruce and Turner 2003). Because the lost pension funds have benefited from tax expenditures that were intended to encourage retirement income security, we propose that the lost pension funds eventually revert to the Social Security Administration OASI Trust Fund. For example, funds that had not been claimed by age 75 would be sent to the Social Security Administration, with provision that they could be claimed at a later date from Social Security if the claimant was found. This proposal would strengthen the funding of Social Security, and it would assure that the funds were used for their intended purpose of enhancing retirement income security. It would also provide a central place for people to contact when looking for lost accounts.

LESSONS FOR THE UNITED STATES

Finding a lost pension is much more difficult in the United States than in the United Kingdom or Australia. In the United States with decentralized records that are not designed for tracing pensions, workers and people searching on their behalf may need to contact a number of different sources of information and ultimately fail to find a lost pension. In the United Kingdom and Australia, by contrast, workers need only contact a single source specifically designed for assisting them in finding a lost pension. The Australian approach maintains a central registry, as in the United Kingdom, but the registry contains information about workers as well as information about plans.

Although we live in the Information Age, the problems discussed here are largely problems of information management. The experience of the United Kingdom and Australia suggests the following lessons.

Lesson One. A centralized system for tracking pension plans needs to be established to help all pension participants.

Lesson Two. The Form 5500 could be modified to include a lost participant form that would be the basis for a lost participant registry. Plans could be required to indicate as lost participants for whom it has had two mailings returned.

Lesson Three. In Australia, the government is instituting a system where it will contact workers with lost accounts. Such a system could be instituted in the United States with the IRS contacting workers with lost accounts who had filed income tax returns.

Lesson Four. The search approach in Australia provides the worker four search options, including searching on-line.

Lesson Five. Based on the experience in the United Kingdom, the annual cost of maintaining a tracing service for finding pension plans and assisting participants would be about $26 million. This is a rough estimate that does not take into account cost savings that would occur due to efficiencies in replacing search activities that already occur. A lower-cost option would be to use the approach in Australia, where workers have the option of searching on-line.

Lesson Six. Having lost pension accounts sent to the Social Security Administration would assure that the money was used for the purpose of providing retirement security. It would also facilitate people looking for lost accounts finding the money, since they would have a central place to contact.

Lesson Seven. Effort should be made to prevent lost pensions from occurring. For example, when W2 tax forms are sent out from former employers, there could be the requirement to also provide information about pensions with former employers.

REFERENCES

Australian Government, The Treasury. 2013a. "Reforms to Make the Superannuation System Fairer." http://ministers.treasury.gov.au/Display Docs.aspx?doc=pressreleases/2013/020.htm&pa geID=003& min= brs& Year=&DocType

Australian Government. 2013b. "Super Fund Lookup." http://super fundlookup.gov.au/

Australian Tax Office. 2013. "SuperSeeker." http://www.ato.gov.au/Calculators-andtools/SuperSeeker/

BBC. 2010. "Thousands Reclaim Lost Pensions." October 12. http://www.bbc.co.uk/news/business-11523295

Blake, David and Turner, John A. 2002. "ISO Lost Pensions." *Contingencies* March/April, pp. 72-74.

Blake, David and Turner, John A. 2002. "Lost Pensions and Lost Pensioners." *Benefits Quarterly* 18(3) Third Quarter, pp. 51-64 (with David Blake).

Blake, David and Turner, John A. 2001. "Lost Pensions, Lost Pensioners: Is a National Registry of Pension Plans the Answer?" Pensions Institute Discussion Paper. http://www.retirementplanblog.com/wp0113.pdf

Bruce, Ellen A. and Turner, John A. 2003. "Let Lost Retirement Money Revert to Social Security." *Contingencies* May-June: 26-29.

Bruce, Ellen A. and Turner, John A. 2004. "Lost Pension Money: Who is Responsible? Who Benefits?" *John Marshall Law Review* 37(3) (Spring): 695-726.

Bruce, Ellen A.; Turner, John A. and Lee, Dongsoo. 2005. "Lost Pensions: An Empirical Investigation." *Benefits Quarterly* 2005, vol. 21(1).

Government of the United Kingdom. 2013. "Find a Lost Pension." https://www.gov.uk/find-lostpension

Shury, Jan and Koerbitz, Christoph. 2010. "The Pension Tracing Service: A Quantitative Research Study to Establish Who is Using the Service, and Their Outcomes." Department for Work and Pensions, Research Report

No. 697. http://research.dwp.gov.uk/asd/asd5/rports2009- 2010/rrep697. pdf

Turner, John A. 2012. "Lost Pension Registries in the U.K. and Australia." Pension Rights Center. http://www.pensionrights.org/publications/fact-sheet/lost-pension-plan-registries-uk-andaustralia

Turner, John A. 2007. "Wider Net is Cast for Lost Pensions." *AARP Bulletin,* March, p. 4.

U.S. Department of Labor, Employee Benefits Security Administration. 2012. "Private Pension Plan Bulletin: Abstract of 2010 Form 5500 Annual Reports." http://www.dol.gov/ebsa/PDF/2010pensionplanbulletin.PDF

INDEX

G

H

I

J

L

S

T

U

V

W